In classic John Schu fashion, *The Gift*  impact stories have on children, for the home, and for our hearts. Joh strategies and resources to build a robust, diverse, and intentional library. *The Gift of Story* is a heartfelt literary love letter to all the emphatic, enthusiastic, and empathetic readers who impact the reading lives of children.

 Alice Lee, ED.D., Elementary Principal and Director of Diversity, Equity, and Inclusion

This is just the book my heart needed! *The Gift of Story* takes a dive into the affective benefits that reading can bring ALL readers. You'll learn how stories can heal hearts and minds, inspire change and growth, clarify perspectives, build compassion, and connect all readers together. Don't miss out on this very special and beautiful celebration of literacy.

 Becky Calzada, Library Coordinator, Leander ISD, Texas

John Schu's *The Gift of Story* resonates with my librarian heart. This book serves as a reminder that connecting, inspiring, and motivating students to read is an important and sacred job. Mr. Schu weaves together educators working in various roles to share a plethora of ideas, inspirations, and stories to build up literacy in a learning community. *The Gift of Story* is all about the heart. Thank you, John, for sharing your heart so we can make connections with all the hearts we serve as educators and librarians.

 Tamiko Brown, SLJ School Librarian of the Year 2017

The Gift of Story will remind educators why we do this work. My heart needed this book. In the spirit of Mr. Schu, I want to buy this book for every educator I know.

 Colby Sharp, Fifth-Grade Teacher and Co-Founder of the Nerdy Book Club

John Schu is every educator's librarian. With his inspiring connections and cherished insight, he shines a light on the right story for every reader. This gifted storyteller has penned his magic to the page and it's exactly what all our 'book hearts' need.

Ali Schilpp, SLJ School Librarian of the Year 2019

John Schu has an innate ability to connect readers with the book their heart needs—this time, he's written it. *The Gift of Story* equips educators to share their heart through story; to nurture connections among our readers and stories that extend beyond the academic elements to also include the affective ones that change readers, their hearts, and the world.

Elisabeth Stayer, Librarian and Educator

John Schu is a legendary presenter for a reason—his love of books and literacy inspires educators and students around the globe. *The Gift of Story* is a John Schu presentation in book form. It's uplifting. It's motivating. It's life-affirming. Happy reading!

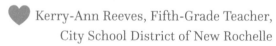 Travis Jonker, Elementary School Librarian,
Wayland Union Schools (MI)

The Gift of Story by John Schu is indeed a gift to hearts everywhere. It covers the importance of dialogue, questions, and basic human experiences as they relate to reading. Then ultimately how they connect to the heart of the reader. This book will rejuvenate the hearts of educators and all who read it while developing spaces for all readers to share their love of stories.

Kerry-Ann Reeves, Fifth-Grade Teacher,
City School District of New Rochelle

Happy Reading!

The Gift of Story

Exploring the Affective Side of the Reading Life

John Schu

John Schu

Stenhouse
PUBLISHERS

Portsmouth, New Hampshire

Stenhouse

PUBLISHERS

www.stenhouse.com

Stenhouse Publishers
www.stenhouse.com

Library of Congress Cataloging-in-Publication Data
Names: Schu, John, 1981– author.
Title: The gift of story : exploring the affective side of the reading life
   / John Schu.
Description: Portsmouth, New Hampshire : Stenhouse Publishers, 2022. |
   Includes bibliographical references and index. |
Identifiers: LCCN 2021034018 (print) | LCCN 2021034019 (ebook) | ISBN
   9781625312082 (paperback) | ISBN 9781625312099 (ebook)
Subjects: LCSH: Reading (Elementary) | Reading—Psychology of. |
   Storytelling in education. | Affective education.
Classification: LCC LB1573 .S336 2022 (print) | LCC LB1573 (ebook) | DDC
   372.4—dc23
LC record available at https://lccn.loc.gov/2021034018
LC ebook record available at https://lccn.loc.gov/2021034019

Cover design by Cindy Butler
Interior design and typesetting by Gina Poirier

Printed in the United States of America
This book is printed on paper certified by third-party standards for sustainably
managed forestry.
28 27 26 25 24 23 22   4371 9 8 7 6 5 4 3 2 1

For Dr. Penny Britton Kolloff, who showed me
the power of story and the importance of self-care
by sharing Sharon Creech and Harry Bliss's
A Fine, Fine School with me in 2001.

For teacher-librarians, who create spaces
and places that advocate for children
and deliver joy and love
through story.

Contents

Foreword

by Katherine Applegate

Most forewords don't open with a confession. Nonetheless, I feel I should admit this up front: I've always been a bit jealous of John Schu.

It all goes back to a mutual friend of ours. Big guy, name of Ivan. Silver hair. Endearing grin. Banana fan.

Ivan was many things. Traveler. Prisoner. Artist. Symbol.

Also: Gorilla.

Here's how it started. In 2012, I published a children's novel called *The One and Only Ivan,* and John was one of its earliest and kindest champions. He even embarked on a summer road trip with his dear friend, Donna Kouri, to Zoo Atlanta, in order to meet the real Ivan, the western lowland gorilla whose story had inspired my book. I was so touched by John's enthusiasm that I sent along a small plush toy gorilla, along with baseball caps and key chains emblazoned with "Let's Go South '12: Two Friends, a Gorilla, and a Map."

After a meandering route, they made it to Atlanta. Sure enough, John and Donna, along with the terrific writer, Laurel Snyder, were able to spend time behind the scenes with Ivan. Dressed in surgical garb (to protect Ivan's health), they got to see the breathtaking majesty of a silverback gorilla up close. To gaze into those wise and long-suffering eyes. To watch him peel, in his meticulous Ivan way, an orange.

The best part? John had a copy of *The One and Only Ivan* with him. And Ivan actually "signed" the book with his paint-covered thumbprint.

Just a few weeks later, Ivan passed away. He was fifty, remarkably old by gorilla standards, and the zoo held a memorial service for him. People came from all over the world to pay their respects to the primate who'd taught us so much about how to care for captive wild animals.

I'd never attended a gorilla funeral before, but it was a glorious day, and I was glad I could be there. It was bittersweet, to be sure; I'd spent so much time imagining Ivan's inner life, without ever actually being able to meet him. But that was a tiny thing, compared to the huge outpouring of love I witnessed.

To this day, I remain a little jealous that John got to hang out with Ivan. But it's awfully hard to nurse a grudge when someone tells you that you've written the book of their heart. And when that someone is Mr. Schu, well . . . there simply are no words to express how much that means. (Something you rarely hear from a writer.)

That's the thing about John. When he loves a book, he loves it wholeheartedly. And it's that zeal—that boundless, effervescent energy—you are about to discover in the pages that follow.

Spoiler alert: This book will change you.

It will enlarge your soul. It will open your heart the way the sun coaxes a bud into bloom. You will come away feeling renewed, hopeful, energized, connected.

That's promising a lot of a book and asking a lot of its author.

But perhaps you've never met Mr. Schu. What you remember most, when you walk away from an encounter with John, is his infectious, joyful love of books. His warmth. His smile.

To tell the truth, I wondered if John's sparkling exuberance could possibly translate to the page. If you've been lucky enough to watch John interact with educators or students, you know what I mean. He gives out books like a literary Johnny Appleseed. His booktalk audiences are as fervent and devoted as diehard Marvel fans.

When John Schu loves a book, you can't help but love it, too.

How do you make that kind of in-person magic happen on the page? Somehow John does it. He recreates the same delight and wonder and love for story that you feel in his presence. It's like you're chatting over a cup of coffee with your dearest friend about a book that changed your life.

Teachers, librarians, media specialists, administrators, and parents will find a wealth of fun and practical ways to encourage the love of reading. John has curated amazing insights from authors and teachers alike, while mining his own vast experience as a teacher-librarian, professor, and author.

Most importantly, again and again, he reminds us about the affective side of reading. John doesn't just suggest timely and engaging books (although your "to be read" pile will be towering by the time you finish reading this). He suggests ways to use stories to heal, to inspire, to clarify, to teach compassion, and to connect.

He reminds us that stories matter because connection matters. Because, as he says, matching the right child with the right book is a "sacred task."

How perfect that this book is called *The Gift of Story*. Because it is a gift. You will read this and come away inspired. And you will return to it, again and again, to buoy your spirits when the work, as it will, gets hard.

When you feel lost in the black hole of test scores and Zoom meetings, in crises big and small, in challenged titles and tight budgets, this book will be your touchstone. For every teacher and librarian and parent who's placed the right book in the right hands at the right time, *The Gift of Story* is a reminder that you are not just molding minds, you are nurturing souls.

What a gift you are giving each day when you look at a child and say, "I think this story might speak to you."

And what a gift you have been given with this book.

KATHERINE APPLEGATE
Los Angeles, California

A Note from John

Dear Reader,

One of my favorite experiences traveling from conference to conference, from school to school, from event to event, is connecting with students, teacher-librarians, classroom teachers, administrators, and families through story. Hearing their stories. Sharing my own. And, of course, talking about books and authors and sharing their stories.

I feel so connected in spontaneous, fly-by-the-seat-of-your-pants moments like this. I thrive on the unknown, the different, and the unexpected. And speaking with hundreds of people at a time is the perfect place for these conditions. There is an ever-changing audience and energy, oh, wondrous energy, permeating my soul and my heart. This is where I feel most at home.

Of course, replicating that experience on the page requires a different energy. A challenge that, honestly, terrifies me. I'm more comfortable when I'm with you in real life. It feels spontaneous. The page is forever.

Still, I want you to know that this is a book of my heart. In it, I'll share thoughts, recommendations, stories, and the interactions I've had with thousands and thousands and thousands of students and educators over the past twenty years. And, even as I write—without the energy of a live audience providing input, guiding the conversation, and filling the room and my heart with joy—I will imagine you are sitting beside me as we take this journey together, working tirelessly to create environments in which all children interact with teachers, teacher-librarians, and administrators who read to them, booktalk with them, and view them not as labels but as individuals who need to be surrounded with authentic literature, given opportunities to discuss, debate, connect, laugh, and cry over stories—and experience buckets and buckets of love.

Through our shared story, we'll imagine a world in which every child enters a classroom or a school library to find enthusiastic literacy champions waiting to go on the most excellent and exciting reading journeys together—waiting to recommend that special book that stays with them for the rest of their lives. Let's imagine ourselves as champions willing and excited to go on these journeys through story.

Speaking of journeys and stories, it's about time to get ours started.

Are you ready?

Happy reading 💜

John Sch

Book of Your Heart

I'm not sure there is a better, more comforting balm for the heart than celebrating books and connecting through stories. With this mission in mind, I travel the world collecting and sharing the stories of the students, educators, taxi drivers, servers, and fellow travelers I meet while advocating for the reading lives of children and spreading book joy. I work with over 50,000 kids every school year and love visiting with them, booktalking titles I'm excited about, and learning about which books an auditorium filled with third graders thinks everyone should know about.

Is there a book that changed your life?

Is there a book that feels like a best friend to you?

Is there a book you have read so many times that most of it is tattooed on your heart?

Is there a book you think everyone in this room should know about?

Is there a book that calms you and helps you find your way back to joy?

Is there a book that helped you better understand yourself or a classmate?

Is there a book you wish you could give to everyone you meet?

These are questions I often ask students when we visit. During our time together, we discuss how powerful it feels when a book opens our hearts. We talk about how reading is a workout for our imaginations and discuss how stories can make our hearts bigger and more open. These exchanges help everyone in the room learn more about themselves as readers and often lead to the best spontaneous booktalks. I always love these conversations, because when we talk about books, you can instantly feel everyone connecting. It's a magical moment, almost like electricity, when someone shares why and how a specific book touched their heart. This sharing always seems to bring us closer together, growing our hearts and community.

#StoryIs

"Story is inside all of us."

ERIN ENTRADA KELLY, AUTHOR
OF MAYBE MAYBE MARISOL RAINEY

I tell everyone who will listen about the day Katherine Applegate's (2012) *The One and Only Ivan* changed my life. It may surprise you to think that a children's book could have such an impact on my adult self, but *Ivan* spoke to me in a way that few books had up to that point. There was something about this book, this character, and the way Applegate's words reached from the page to draw me in, connecting Ivan's story to mine, linking us in an inexplicable way. In essence, it touched my soul and became a forever book of my heart.

I read *The One and Only Ivan* on December 27, 2011, and remember feeling as though I was glued to the book. This fictional tale of a real-life shopping mall gorilla, who discovers the healing power of friendship, went everywhere with me—into the kitchen when I needed a drink of water, into the bathroom, to the kitchen table. I could feel my heart and soul expanding. Perhaps you've had similar experiences, books you couldn't put down. Books that made you anxious to think they would end all too soon. That feeling of having twenty pages left. Of having to say goodbye. Of the end.

Ivan's story moved me on such a personal level that I began to share his book with everyone I could. I blogged about it. I wrote about it. I took a literary road trip, traveling the country sharing Ivan's story, and eventually got to meet the real Ivan in person. Still, what was it about this book? This story? This character? As a reader, teacher, and school librarian, I'd read thousands of books by that point. What was it about this particular book that spoke to me?

#StoryIs

"Story is something constantly tumbling around in my brain. I daydream all the time and tend to get frustrated when the real world pulls me out of my imagination. I'm glad that being a writer and putting my distractions down on paper lets me pretend to be productive."

ADRIANNA CUEVAS, AUTHOR OF CUBA IN MY POCKET

In hindsight, I realize that Ivan's story spoke to me in a private, quiet way. As I was reading it, I started to understand parts of myself. His experiences through struggles, loss, survival, friendship, and hope are universal stories that, when shared through the heart, connect us all. I experienced a catharsis of sorts through reading it, as I'm sure many of you have. And, while *Ivan* went on to win the 2013 Newbery Medal, I went on to elevate and celebrate more stories like it that helped me share my heart and inspired others through similar experiences.

The Heart of Story

At the end of my school visits, I'm always excited when a group of children comes over to talk about their favorite books, stories, and authors, often sharing books of their own hearts. I'll never forget when fourth grader Mario approached me, a bit shy and nervous. He seemed unsure and kept rotating himself to the end of the line, not wanting to share in front of the others. He thanked me for talking about *The One and Only Ivan* and for sharing that it made me cry. "I read it last year," he said. "It made me cry a lot." We talked about how sadness in books can help us better deal with sadness in our own lives and better prepare us for difficult moments in life. "I know sadness," he said. "My sister died last year. Books helped me. Ivan helped me." My heart was full when I left that meeting. Full of grief for his loss, but also full from the connection our hearts made through sharing Ivan's experience—and through that, our own. When we create conditions where children are safe to experience life through the lens of characters and their struggles and successes, books can be a bridge to connect and restore us.

Stories have the power to strengthen and heal hearts. A teacher-librarian put *The One and Only Ivan* in Mario's hands, but probably had no idea, when they did so, that they were also tattooing love and light and laughter and hope on his heart. Or maybe they did, and that's exactly why they did it. A book often walks into our lives when we need it the most. Matching children with books is one of the most important roles we have as educators. It's a sacred task. We connect with students on a different level when we share how a book resonates with us—when we share what it feels and looks like when a book leads to a catharsis. When we speak about books from the heart, students start to internalize these messages as encouragement to speak from the heart as well.

Have you ever read a book you knew would go directly from your heart into your classroom? A book you couldn't wait to experience with your students? If you have, then you already know what it's like to find a book of your heart. In the coming pages, we'll explore how sharing our hearts through story in this way—in the way you share books with your readers, in the way Ivan spoke to me—can help us build stronger learning communities, connect to others in our world, and understand ourselves as readers and individuals in new and exciting ways.

What Is Story?

Every child who walks into your classroom or library has a story. But how do we establish opportunities for them to tell their stories and find themselves in the stories of others? When we share our hearts in authentic ways, we inspire those around us to do the same. Before we can discuss what it means to share our hearts through story, it might be helpful to establish what we mean by the word *story*. If you think about it, the way a third-grade teacher defines story is probably different from how a music teacher defines story. The way a music teacher defines story is probably different from how a teacher-librarian defines story. And the way a teacher-librarian defines story is probably different from how a fourth grader defines story. Since we all have our own personal definitions of the word, take a moment to reflect on how you define story.

Perhaps your definition brings to mind story elements like main idea, theme, characters, setting, and plot. These are all very important in the literacy work we do with children, but we can expand our idea of story as we consider other elements that may not be immediately evident—such as joy, happiness, compassion, laughter, connection, culture, and identity. For our purposes, we'll apply a flexible definition that makes room for story to meet both the academic and affective needs of our students (see Figure 1.1). Sharing your heart through story is a way to bring

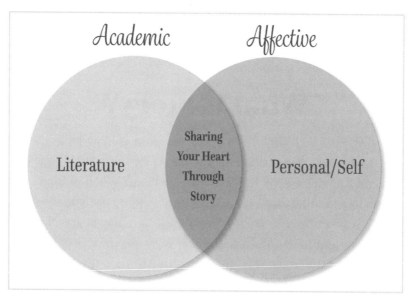

FIGURE 1.1

more of the affective side into our students' reading lives. So while you'll definitely see academic elements throughout this book, we'll focus largely on what is often missing—the affective.

When we share our hearts through story, we create environments in which children can feel warm and safe and loved. I've witnessed again and again how students open up their hearts to teachers and each other when we share how a story allowed us to view the world in new ways, healed our hearts, and inspired us to take action. As we further refine our understanding of story, we'll bring our lens into deeper focus on its affective elements.

🌀 *Story as* Clarifier

This helps us individually and in groups answer questions about our heart's deepest wonderings and passions. Think of the animal lover who checks out every caring for a pet book or the junior historian who can't get enough of Kate Messner's History Smashers series.

⊕ *Story as* Healer

This helps our heart work through difficult experiences as well as internal and external conflicts. Think of the child who deals with the loss of a grandparent by reading Caron Levis and Charles Santoso's (2016) *Ida, Always* every day or the middle schooler who, after reading Jen Petro Roy's (2019) *Good Enough*, admits to himself and a family member that he has an eating disorder and needs help.

🌐 *Story as* Inspiration

This helps us explore and discover our passions. Think of the child who folds hundreds of origamis after reading Tom Angleberger's (2010) *The Strange Case of Origami Yoda* or the child who becomes an activist for something important to them after reading *Marley Dias Gets It Done: And So Can You* (Dias 2018).

🌱 *Story as* Compassion

This helps us understand ourselves and others. Think of the child who develops more empathy after reading Jacqueline Woodson and Rafael López's (2018) *The Day You Begin* or the adolescent who comes to terms with her sexuality after reading Ashley Herring Blake's (2018) *Ivy Aberdeen's Letter to the World*.

🌍 *Story as* Connector

When Kate DiCamillo (Library of Congress 2014) was the National Ambassador for Young People's Literature, she said, "Together, we see the world. Together, we see one another. We connect. And when we connect, we are changed." Stories answer this call by helping us open our hearts and connect. Think about times when everyone in a community comes together to celebrate a book or when every fifth grader has tears running down their faces after their teacher reads aloud the last sentence in John David Anderson's (2017) *Ms. Bixby's Last Day*.

#StoryIs

"Story is the way we make Truth portable. It's difficult to transmit the deepest part of ourselves in words alone, the part we normally share by spending a day together. But in story-form, those parts of our hearts can grow little feet and can scurry long distances—or they can crawl slow and steady into the world."

M. EVAN WOLKENSTEIN, AUTHOR OF *TURTLE BOY*

In addition to these five affective elements of story, story can serve as *windows, mirrors, and sliding glass doors.* In her seminal 1990 article, Dr. Rudine Sims Bishop wrote, "Books are sometimes windows, offering views of worlds that may be real or imagined, familiar or strange. These windows are also sliding glass doors, and readers have only to walk through in imagination to become part of whatever world has been created and recreated by the author. When lighting conditions are just right, however, a window can also be a mirror. Literature transforms human experience and reflects it back to us, and in that reflection we can see our own lives and experiences as part of the larger human experience." As you reflect on the five affective elements of story presented here, what connections to Sims Bishop's work can you make? How can seeing books through the lens of mirrors, windows, and sliding glass doors inform our understanding of the ways story acts to clarify, connect, heal, inspire, and teach us?

Consider these five affective elements as you think back on the way Mario and I connected through our separate encounters with *The One and Only Ivan.* Even though I didn't know his whole experience, we were able to make many unspoken connections through Ivan's story—both shared and individual. In this small and poignant tale, we both found *clarity* around our individual struggles; *connected* with Ivan, Stella, Ruby, Bob, Julia, and each other; better *understood* and *articulated* our own grief; and were *inspired* to share how Ivan's tenacity, strength, and precision of language helped us start the *healing* process. This is the gift of story. This is the power of a book going directly from our heart into our classrooms.

This can happen outside of our familiar school settings as well. How many times have you connected with others through the experience of having read the same book? For instance, have you ever spotted a stranger reading one of your favorite books on a train or in a park and felt somehow instantly closer to them? Even when we come from different backgrounds, different perspectives, or different generations, story has the power to bring us together, to change us, to open our eyes, and to engage us in shared experiences through narratives. Dr. Susan Tan (2018) writes, "Story is so important. Stories are how we communicate, how we get to know each other, how we practice empathy and compassion, and how we broaden our imaginations and senses of who we are and who we can be." Whether we are in a large group or an intimate one-on-one setting, stories have a way to reach across hearts and connect us.

At this point, take a moment to reflect on what all this means for you and the work you do with children. Does it resonate with your mindset? Perhaps you've seen the effects of connecting through story firsthand as a reader, teacher, or teacher-librarian. Essentially, when hearts connect, brains expand and communities are healed. Sharing connections through books can help us understand universal truths about ourselves and others. You don't have to be a shopping mall gorilla to feel trapped, a bus-driving pigeon to long for your heart's desire, or a writing spider to understand the value of friendship.

Stories affirm our experiences. They challenge our comfort zone. They give us space to hibernate and pull us out of our isolation when we need to be reminded we aren't alone. They help us evolve. They feed our human existence. In the following chapters, we'll explore how stories can change us, inspire us, connect us to others, answer our deepest questions, and help us heal. We'll look at ways sharing our hearts through literacy can help us celebrate, tell, define, revise, and imagine our own stories and how experiencing other people's stories can connect us through universal truths. And, we'll do all of this while shining particular light on the important role books and libraries in our communities play to help us connect across stories.

Story as Healer

"I hope my story helps you to live more fully into your own." This is the final sentence of Nikki Grimes's (2019) author's note in *Ordinary Hazards: A Memoir*. That sentence has been bouncing around inside of my head for months. I've been thinking about how painful, albeit *healing*, it must have been for Nikki to write about growing up with a mother with paranoid schizophrenia, spending years in the foster care system, being separated from her sister, and experiencing sexual trauma. Putting her truth and heart on the page allowed her to face the painful moments of her childhood.

Writing stories can heal us.

And I can't stop thinking about the readers who will see pieces of themselves in her memoir and start to tell and own their stories; they will begin to heal.

Reading stories can heal us.

Even if your mother doesn't suffer from mental illness and you've never experienced sexual trauma, you can start to understand the internal struggles Nikki went through. You don't have to live Nikki's life for her story to help heal yours.

Sharing stories can heal us.

Inviting conversations with students that require the level of intimacy needed to heal through story requires a great deal of trust. We must create warm, safe, loving, and trusting environments. It's difficult to be vulnerable in relationships in which we are unsure—in relationships lacking trust. If we take this directly to our learning communities, we're prompted to reflect on the steps we have taken to create loving environments that support sharing our hearts in a healing way.

But how often do we consider the ways our environments and interactions send messages of support and create healing spaces? I'm reminded of an experience a friend and I recently had in a new neighborhood coffee shop. When we ordered, we were surprised to

PHOTOGRAPH BY ELAINE FREITAS

#StoryIs

"Story is everything. Stories are how I escape from reality, but also how I process my own life. I wrote Watercress because I had a memory that felt pivotal in my life, but I didn't know how or why. The act of writing it was cathartic—it allowed me to let go of a lot of resentment and guilt."

ANDREA WANG, AUTHOR OF WATERCRESS

find that there wasn't a menu posted behind the counter. Paper menus weren't available either. And even though the barista was cheerful and helpful, we couldn't shake this odd feeling that we were somehow less welcome in this environment.

What are the hidden messages or assumptions that help us feel important or included?

During my three years as a children's bookseller at Barnes & Noble, I learned a lot of valuable lessons about customer service and connecting with others—lessons that carried over into my classroom and school library. Consider these two scenarios.

Scenario 1

CUSTOMER: I am looking for *A Single Shard*.
ME: You'll find it in the Newbery section. (*I point toward the Newbery section.*)

Scenario 2

CUSTOMER: I am looking for *A Single Shard*.
ME: Oh, I love Linda Sue Park's *A Single Shard*. I've read it twice. I cheered so loudly when it received the 2002 Newbery Medal.
CUSTOMER: My son's school librarian booktalked it last week. He's excited to read it, but there's a long hold list for it in the library. He begged me to buy him a copy.
(*We walk to the Newbery section. I pull the book off the shelf and place it in his hands.*)
ME: May I help you find anything else?
CUSTOMER: Do you have any recommendations for a sixth grader who loves poetry?
ME: Are you familiar with *Locomotion* by Jacqueline Woodson? (*The conversation continues, sharing books and recommendations.*)

As you read through this exchange, consider the ways the second situation is more welcoming and invites a deeper, more meaningful conversation about books and reading. We can look for connections like this in our school environments, as well, as we monitor how we share excitement and energy around reading. Take a minute to reflect on your own learning community and think about the energy and conversations you see around books. How are students welcomed to a safe, loving environment? In what ways do we exemplify this through our words and actions?

For instance, as students enter a literacy-related assembly or celebration, observe how they interact with one another, how teachers interact with students, how teachers interact with each other, and how the principal interacts with students and teachers. Are the children holding books? Are the teachers sharing excitement about reading? Do you hear booktalks? Do people look excited to be in the space? Do hearts seem open? Or do they feel closed? Do the people look sad and lonely and in need of a spoonful of joy? The more we observe our environments through the lens of creating warm, safe, and loving experiences, the more we become aware of the connections we make and the effects they have.

At an assembly a few years ago, I met a fifth grader who was carrying a notebook as though it was a chest filled with gold. It looked like a lifeline, a best friend. When I asked him about his notebook, he showed me his comics, sketches, doodles, short stories. His face brightened as he turned pages, taking me on a tour of his notebook and sharing his stories with me. He asked if I had a notebook, and I readily shared mine with him. As he walked away, writing in his

#StoryIs

"Story is magic. Stories are the way I make sense of our messy and complicated world. The stories we tell about others and ourselves have enormous power to change and shape our lives. When you really think about it, all of us are a walking collection of stories."

JASMINE WARGA, AUTHOR OF *THE SHAPE OF THUNDER*

#StoryIs

"Story is what saved me as a child. I grew up with ADHD and dyslexia, and I didn't want to be known as 'the kid who misbehaves' or 'the kid who can't read well,' so I began creating my own stories. Writing and drawing stories as a kid gave me a necessary creative outlet and a new identity."

DAV PILKEY, AUTHOR OF THE DOG MAN AND CAPTAIN UNDERPANTS SERIES

notebook with intense focus and purpose, he looked happy and his heart seemed open, but I noticed that his teacher didn't seem so pleased. A few moments later, his teacher demanded the notebook and pointed to his seat. You could see in his eyes the need to resist and then, realizing it wouldn't matter, he gave in. My heart broke. I thought of Caldecott Honor artist Dav Pilkey, the bestselling author of *The Adventures of Captain Underpants* (1997) and *Dog Man* (2016).

About ten minutes after the teacher took away his notebook, I shared Dav Pilkey's story about how he created the characters of Captain Underpants and Dog Man when he was in the second grade. His teachers, librarian, and administrators didn't understand his ADHD and dyslexia, nor did they appreciate his talents. One day, his teacher ripped up his Captain Underpants comics and told him to stop wasting his time on silly stories and silly drawings. You could hear gasps throughout the room. I glanced at the fifth grader who had just experienced a similar message and his face lit up. His joy returned, and I could tell that, by connecting with Dav's story, he had begun to *heal* in some way.

Now, we can never know why his teacher reacted to his notebook in that way. I'm sure there's a backstory we're not aware of. But take a moment and reflect on this scenario. How often do we let distractions get in the way and misinterpret situations in a less than healing way? We are in the business of taking care of hearts. We are in the business of listening. We are in the business of helping hearts grow and connect.

#StoryIs

"Story is power, joy, magic, the feeling of flying through the sky on the back of a winged pakkhiraj horse! For me, a daughter of Indian immigrants growing up in America, reading helped me find my strength and a sense of my own voice and my own place in the world."

SAYANTANI DASGUPTA, AUTHOR OF *FORCE OF FIRE*

From the Brain to the Heart

How do we know if a school is a safe, warm, and loving space for sharing our stories? What does healing through stories look like? What does it sound like? What does it feel like? Dr. Sayantani DasGupta is known in the world of children's literature as the author of the Kiranmala and the Kingdom Beyond series. But, she was originally trained in pediatrics and currently teaches courses in narrative medicine at the Center for the Study of Ethnicity and Race and the Institute for Comparative Literature and Society at Columbia University. Dr. DasGupta (2014) defines narrative medicine as "the clinical and scholarly movement to honor the central role of story in healthcare." On her website she shares

According to a study conducted at the University of Sussex in 2009, reading for as little as six minutes per day can reduce your stress level by up to 68 percent. Neuroscientist Dr. David Lewis, one of the researchers, said in The Telegraph *(Lewis, et al. 2009), "Losing yourself in a book is the ultimate relaxation. It really doesn't matter what book you read, by losing yourself in a thoroughly engrossing book you can escape from the worries and stresses of the everyday world and spend a while exploring the domain of the author's imagination."*

that she spends her life at the intersection of the stethoscope and the pen. When she was in practice as a pediatrician in the South Bronx and Northern Manhattan, she wrote prescriptions for reading. She would give her patients books to take home, but it was often hard to find stories in which a child's own background and family structure were authentically represented and celebrated. Dr. DasGupta (2018) wrote an incredibly powerful piece for Scholastic Book Fairs' *Reader Leader* blog called "Stories Are Good Medicine: Literacy, Health, and Representation." In it she shares, "Being deprived of stories about people like you, or being deprived of stories about people in community with you, is not simply unfair or unjust, it is deeply unhealthy." She wrote *The Serpent's Secret* (2018) (Book 1 in the Kiranmala and the Kingdom Beyond series) with this in mind—she wanted all kids to know they are worthy of starring in their own story. Dr. DasGupta ends the blog post with one of the most thought-provoking and important passages I have ever read:

> *Health, in its fullest definition, is a sense of wholeness—an ability to move through this world knowing you and yours are loved, valued, and celebrated. Librarians (not to mention teachers, coaches, neighbors, friends—anyone who has the opportunity to share stories and celebrate reading with young people) are then also in the business of health. Stocking, reading, sharing, recommending, and celebrating stories in which all our children can see themselves are practices of healing, a way to write a healthier future for our world into being.*

You can read Dr. DasGupta's full blog post, "Stories Are Good Medicine: Literacy, Health, and Representation," and find out more about her work here:

Spend some time with that statement. Let it marinate. We are in the business of health. We can take care of our students' hearts and health by making sure our classrooms and libraries are filled with stories that allow our students to see themselves authentically reflected on the page. Books that invite healing through connected stories.

Voices From

THE WRITER'S DESK

As we continue to consider story as healing, we also recognize that writers often bring their own stories to the page in an act of healing for themselves and others. You may know actor and activist Maulik Pancholy as Jonathan from NBC's *30 Rock* or as the voice of Baljett Tjinden on *Phineas and Ferb*. He's also a children's book author with a unique take on the importance of seeing ourselves in stories and how doing so can heal our hearts. His debut middle-grade novel, *The Best at It* (2019), tells the story of Rahul Kapoor, an Indian American middle schooler who is beginning to realize he might be gay.

Maulik Pancholy

I loved reading books as a kid. I still do. But growing up, I never saw characters who looked like me in the books I read, let alone kids who were dealing with the things I was dealing with. I think seeing a kid of color grappling with his sexual identity and the anxieties of feeling "different"—on multiple levels—would have made me feel a little less alone in the world.

It's vital for young people to see their stories reflected back in the books they read and in the television shows and movies they watch.

As an actor, I'm very conscious of this. I know firsthand that when you don't see yourself, you can start to question how you fit into the world. Or start to believe you need to be someone you're not. Because you're effectively being told that your story doesn't exist, that it isn't valid, that it doesn't matter. So, I certainly could have used a book like The Best at It in middle school.

The writing process was healing, too. I got to give voice to so many conversations I wished I could have had when I was young. What's been interesting is that the specificity of Rahul's story has also given it universal appeal, just like so many of the books I loved as a kid. I think every child—and adults, too—can relate to feeling different and needing to prove their worth. Sometimes, even to themselves.

You'll notice similar strands of healing across various children's books, as authors share their hearts through stories in ways that, while feeling unique, connect to universal experiences. With this in mind, one of my favorite books to share is Kelly Yang's (2018) *Front Desk*, which is based on her experience of growing up in poverty.

Kelly Yang

As a young immigrant child, I didn't have access to a lot of things that traditionally heal us: therapy, a stable group of friends, health insurance, or a nice home. Instead my life was a constant succession of suitcases, notices from the U.S. Immigration and Naturalization Services to appear at INS, and gunshot sounds that jolted me wide awake at night. My parents and I were first-generation struggling immigrants from China. We moved around a lot, working in motels in some of the toughest neighborhoods in California. I went to eight different schools for eight different grades. At some of these schools, the other kids would tease me about my weird-looking clothes (bought secondhand from a thrift shop) or my small eyes.

Suffice it to say, I was a child in need of a lot of healing. But it was very hard to find when you're moving around so much. I finally found such healing nestled in the pages of borrowed hardback books, the one constant in my life because I always had access to the library. I remember hiding in the library during lunch, crouching in between the aisles, hoping my school librarian wouldn't see me because we weren't really supposed to be in the library at lunch. The librarian, of course, saw me. She came over, smiled at me—no judgment—and handed me a book.

From then on, I went to the library every day. What started out as my sanctuary, the only place I truly felt completely safe, quickly became so much more. Immersed in the pages of a book, I could be anyone. I could run alongside Lucy in Narnia and swim the chocolate lake in Willy Wonka's chocolate factory! It didn't matter that my parents and I worked seven days a week or that the last vacation my family took was coming here to this country—I could travel the world, be anyone, do anything!

Stories have the power to heal because they transcend the boundaries of race, gender, and your current socioeconomic station. They don't care that you add water to your shampoo to make it last longer or that you practice the piano on your desk because you can't afford to buy a real piano. They put all those

differences aside and appeal to what we all have in common—
our emotions, our dreams, and our compassion as human beings.

I am living, walking proof in the power of librarians and stories to heal. And now I am so proud to be giving back by writing
accessible and important books filled with diverse characters
so that all children can see themselves in books. Together, let's
heal the next generation, one child and story at a time!

From the Heart to the Classroom

Everything we've discussed up to this point speaks to that ultimate feeling of when a story connects with yours to help you heal. Think about books that have healed you—books like *Monster* (Myers 1999), *Piecing Me Together* (Watson 2018), *When Stars Are Scattered* (Jamieson and Mohamed 2020), *Fighting Words* (Bradley 2020), *Red, White, and Whole* (LaRocca 2021a), *Flight of the Puffin* (Braden 2021), *Are You There God? It's Me, Margaret* (Blume 1970), and countless others. Likely these stories either made you feel understood or, per- haps, made you feel less alone. They may have helped you find words for what you were feeling or shown you a possible path forward. How can we establish this concept of story as healer explicitly in our classrooms and create situations that implicitly encourage its organic development through interactions within our learning communities?

Sometimes it's easy to forget that we have kids who are struggling on a personal level because it's often such a private thing that we may never know what they're really working through on their own. Because a need for healing speaks to such an internal, personal feeling and because healing often happens on its own timeline, it's not something we can force instructionally. Instead, we create conditions that make it possible for the right book to find the right reader at just the right time. Books can be the perfect prescriptions that let us know we're going to be OK. We give students access to these lifelines and leave room for the magic.

Sharing Our Hearts Through Story Helps Us Feel Understood

One of the best ways we can bring this about in our classrooms and libraries is to be an advocate for stories that validate the uniqueness of each individual already existing in your reading community. During a keynote address, award-winning author Laurie Halse Anderson (2019) said, "I don't write dark stories. I write candles. I write fire." I think about Laurie's wise words often. They remind me of how her powerful and much-needed stories, her candles and fire, have helped so many students heal. Unfortunately, Laurie Halse Anderson's books have appeared multiple times on the American Library Association's Top Banned/Challenged list. People fight to keep her words out of public, school, and classroom libraries. They fight to keep out books that could help so many heal from a variety of similar difficulties and trauma. Author Robin Stevenson was uninvited to a school district in Illinois because a parent complained after learning gay politician and human rights leader Harvey Milk was included in her book *Kid Activists: True Tales of Childhood from Champions of Change* (2019). Tim Federle responded to a librarian who pointed out there weren't any kids in the school like Nate from *Better Nate Than Ever* (2013), a middle school boy coming to terms with being gay, by asking, "Do you have any wizards?" The examples go on and on.

#StoryIs

"Story is a human need, a way to make sense of our lives, our communities, our dreams, and our relationships. It's a catalyst for our imaginations and for healing, learning, connecting, and so much more."

KAELA NOEL, AUTHOR OF *Coo*

What message are we sending to our LGBTQIA+ students who need to belong, students who are struggling with eating disorders, students who are feeling ignored, sidelined, or just plain alone? The books that are censored the most often go missing the most—and they're also the ones our isolated kids seem to need the most. When we purchase, promote, and read aloud books that honor our students' individual journeys, we take an extra step toward creating possibilities for stories to heal their young hearts.

Sharing Our Hearts Through Story Helps Us Feel Less Alone

Another way we can support the healing work of stories is by including titles in our read-alouds and collections that invite readers into a vicariously shared experience. If you've ever processed your own grief while reading Conor's story in *A Monster Calls* (Ness 2011), you know this power firsthand. You know how the right book can help us process difficult feelings and situations and, in turn, help us begin to heal. Do you remember the first time you read *Bridge to Terabithia* (Patterson 1977)? Perhaps, like me, you first experienced it with a group of students. Do you recall the sound the entire room made when the rope snapped? You and your students probably went through the stages of grief together—you likely healed together.

Think of all the stories that draw a direct line to your students' hearts in this way. Whether read privately or shared in larger community groups, coming of age stories like Jasmine Warga's (2019) *Other Words for Home*, books that speak to universal journeys like Lauren Castillo's (2020) *Our Friend Hedgehog*, and characters whose experiences mirror our own and empower us to heal like Ernesto Cisneros' (2020) *Efrén Divided* all invite us to connect to similar experiences and share our own.

Mr. Schu Suggests

Over time, I've collected some great titles that seem to speak to readers and communities in healing ways. In the list that follows, you'll see titles that will bring you joy and make you cry along with stories that will likely leave you contemplating, pondering, and reflecting. As you add your own favorites to this list, look for books that help facilitate conversations about the healing power of story, connect to common experiences within your learning communities, and invite new ways of seeing each other's personal experiences. Recognizing that these are just my suggestions, watch as your students read, and listen in on their responses. Notice what resonates and speaks to them in those just-right healing ways.

💠 *My Heart* by Corinna Luyken

My heart wishes it could give your heart a copy of this beautiful celebration of hearts. It is about taking care of our hearts, acknowledging that sometimes our hearts feel alone, and opening up our hearts to the love that is found around us.

APPLICATION TO STORY AS HEALER

My Heart connects beautifully to Dr. Sayantani DasGupta's work. Use it to facilitate a discussion about how our hearts can be windows, slides, open, closed, broken, shadows, and light. It can be healing and freeing to talk about the status of your heart.

💠 *The End of Something Wonderful: A Practical Guide to a Backyard Funeral* by Stephanie V. W. Lucianovic; illustrated by George Ermos

This humorous and heartfelt book is a guide to saying goodbye to something you love. Readers will appreciate the humor used throughout the

Throughout the pages that follow, I offer lots of suggestions for evergreen books that speak to the heart of the affective elements of story. However, because my list of new gems and instant classics is always growing, check out my regularly updated lists at JohnSchu.com.

story as they learn how to say goodbye and that, although there are similarities in the rituals we go through, we all ultimately say goodbye in our own way.

APPLICATION TO STORY AS HEALER

This book opens conversations about feelings as it validates the wide variety of emotions we may have over losing something or someone precious. This opens the door to discussions of the different emotions children may experience over the same event. It can be used to illustrate there is not one way to be sad; we grieve and show emotions in many different ways.

The Many Colors of Harpreet Singh by Supriya Kelkar; illustrated by Alea Marley

This colorful book made my heart soar. Harpreet shows his moods through the colors of his patka. After a life event makes him feel shy and wanting to wear only white, I found myself cheering him on, along with his parents, hoping he would have the courage to show his colorful self once again. An afterword by Dr. Simran Jeet Singh ties the colors of Harpreet's patka to a simple lesson about Sikhism, allowing the reader a deeper understanding of Harpreet as well as other Sikhs.

APPLICATION TO STORY AS HEALER

Harpreet uses his patka to show when he feels brave, festive, or in need of courage. Use this book to talk about the feelings we all go through: What colors might we choose to express these emotions? We all have a rainbow of emotions; use this book as a springboard to discuss them and help students put a name to them.

Maybe Tomorrow? by Charlotte Agell; illustrated by Ana Ramírez González

Elba carries around a big heavy block, which keeps her from having fun. Norris spends his days dancing around in a cloud of butterflies. Norris befriends Elba and learns that the block she carries is due to the loss of her dear Little Bird. This story is about grief, how it can weigh us down, but how, over time, our friends can help share the burden and in the process make it smaller.

APPLICATION TO STORY AS HEALER

Norris demonstrates how friends can help when we feel sad just by sitting quietly together, by empathizing and listening, and ultimately by helping carry the burden. By doing these things, the sadness lessens. Use this moving picture book to discuss empathy and how it can guide us out of loneliness and help us move forward after a great loss.

The Rabbit Listened by Cori Doerrfeld

Taylor builds a magnificent structure of blocks that is destroyed. Friend after friend comes to console Taylor and give direction as how to solve the problem, yet none of the suggestions appeal to Taylor. Finally, the rabbit comes and doesn't tell Taylor what to do but rather sits with Taylor and listens. This allows Taylor the space to decide how to move forward.

APPLICATION TO STORY AS HEALER

This gentle story is a great springboard to help students learn how to listen. Nobody wants their friend to hurt, and, in an attempt to help, we often fill the air with words and gestures that do anything but help. Through this book, we learn that, often, the best thing we can do when someone is hurting is to sit and listen.

Come with Me by Holly M. McGhee; illustrated by Pascal Lemaître

A child grows frightened as she hears the news and worries about the hatred continuously displayed, so she asks her father and mother what she can do to make the world better. Each parent takes her out and shows her, by example, how small gestures that show bravery and kindness are what make the world better. She takes this lesson to heart and begins to show kindness through simple acts, unaware of how her small act will turn into a great act of beauty, which, ultimately, makes the world better.

Children are easily frightened when faced with negativity. This book helps move away from fear to a place of love and strength as readers realize that simple acts of kindness and bravery can have a domino effect. Brainstorm what simple acts we can do as we decide to take action and start a revolution of our hearts.

Sulwe by Lupita Nyong'O; illustrated by Vashti Harrison

Sulwe and Mich are sisters, yet look nothing alike. Sulwe is envious of her sister, who she thinks is beautiful and popular. She is sure that if her skin were lighter she would find these things, too. Her attempts to become lighter all fail until one night she is transported on a shooting star and learns the story of two similar sisters. She learns that light can only truly shine in the darkest of nights and even the brightest of days need darkness as well.

APPLICATION TO STORY AS HEALER

What a boring world it would be if we were all the same! This book helps students see that beauty comes in many colors and that all are necessary to make our world the wonderful place it is.

Stay: A Girl, a Dog, a Bucket List by Kate Klise; illustrated by M. Sarah Klise

Astrid has never known life without her beloved dog, Eli. As Astrid grows older she realizes that Eli is also growing older only, as happens with dogs, at a much faster pace. Astrid wants to ensure that Eli has experienced life to the fullest and creates a bucket list of adventures for the two of them to make sure.

APPLICATION TO STORY AS HEALER

I want every person who is worried about losing someone dear to experience this book. Life is something to be celebrated. This story is full of hope and love and teaches us not to fear what is coming but, instead, to live every moment full of joy and gratitude. It's not dread and worry that sustain us, but rather the love we show and the memories we create that will last.

◐ *A Map into the World* by Kao Kalia Yang; illustrated by Seo Kim

Paj Ntaub moves into a new home with her family. This book follows the seasons of nature as plants bloom and die and also seasons of life as her mother gives birth, as babies grow, and as a beloved neighbor dies. Paj Ntaub, sad that her neighbor has lost his wife and is alone, creates something very special to help him find his way back into the world again.

APPLICATION TO STORY AS HEALER

Just as there are seasons in nature, there are seasons in life. This is a story to share when students are unsure of changes that are occurring—whether it is moving somewhere new, becoming a sibling, or losing someone dear. Things might be difficult but they progress, and when they are especially hard, our friends can help us find our way again.

◐ *The Scar* by Charlotte Moundlic; illustrated by Olivier Tallec

After a young child's mother dies, they struggle with the myriad of emotions that are brought on by grief. The child struggles to take care of others around them as they earnestly do all they can to keep their mother close.

APPLICATION TO STORY AS HEALER

Death is painful and the grieving process is confusing. This book can foster discussion over the different ways people grieve and the steps we take to keep our loved ones close. It reminds us that, even though a scar remains, the pain will lessen and we can slowly move back to a place of joy.

My favorite titles for story as healer

Story as Inspiration

My heart and ears are always open when I visit classrooms and libraries. I listen. I'm inspired. I take in what students are sharing with each other, what teachers are sharing with students, and what students are sharing with teachers. Nothing quite inspires me more than when children share the books that inspired them to take action, the books that inspired them to create or build something, the books that inspired them to explore and discover new passions, the books that inspired them to look at the world in new and meaningful ways.

As you listen to your own students, tune in to questions like "Have you read . . . ?" and "Will you help me find . . . ?" These are two of the most meaningful questions you'll overhear in a library or a classroom because they illustrate the stories our students find inspirational and, through these interactions, invite us into their story.

Have you read . . .

- 💜 *The Strange Case of Origami Yoda* (Angleberger 2010)? I love nonfiction books about origami. I recently folded 100 origami animals.

- 💜 *Freedom Soup* (Charles 2019)? My family and I made Ti Gran's recipe that's in the back of the book.

- 💜 *Emmy in the Key of Code* (Lucido 2019)? I signed up for a coding class at the public library.

- 💜 *Seashells: More Than a Home* (Stewart 2019)? I researched seashells and started a seashell collection.

Will you help me find . . .

- 💜 a graphic novel that will make me laugh?

- 💜 a two-hankie book?

- 💜 an unputdownable book?

- 💜 a book with characters who go on a journey?

- 💜 a book about dinosaurs?

But how often do we unintentionally douse inspirations? When students make a request, it's important to address this request on a personal level. Chat with them about what piqued their interest. What things specifically make them laugh? Beyond tugging at their hearts, what do they look for in a two-hankie book? Is there a special kind of tension that keeps them turning the pages of a book? Is it the short chapters, the vocabulary, the setting, or something else entirely? If they like books with characters who go on a journey, what part do they enjoy the most—the journey, the challenges they encounter, the people (or animals) they meet along the way? What are their favorite dinosaurs? Do they ever think about studying dinosaurs as a profession in the future? Sometimes in talking with them we realize their initial question needs to be refined. We need to delve deeper. We need to connect with them.

Our readers are people, not statistics. Think about how different those earlier statements and requests are in relation to story when compared with questions like the following:

- I am a level P. Where are the level P books?

- Do you have any books that are fewer than 100 pages?

- Will you help me find a book? My teacher said I am not allowed to read graphic novels or picture books.

- Will you help me find an AR book that is a 3.2 level?

There isn't a lot of inspiration in this second set of questions. Think about the hidden messages we sometimes send in the ways we present story. We all read for different reasons; so do children in our reading communities.

Beyond student interests, inspiration also includes the way stories can move us to take actions in our lives or on behalf of others. Since *Crenshaw*'s (Applegate 2015) release, countless learning communities have been inspired to host food drives and fight childhood hunger. Take a look at the

#StoryIs

"Story is a way to inspire students to dream, to aspire and to envision a life that fulfills one's potential."

SYLVIA ACEVEDO, AUTHOR OF *PATH TO THE STARS: MY JOURNEY FROM GIRL SCOUT TO ROCKET SCIENTIST*

#TeamOctopus hashtag on social media. You'll see how students and teachers around the world have been inspired to speak out against gun violence, domestic abuse, and childhood poverty after reading Ann Braden's (2018) *The Benefits of Being an Octopus*. Some teachers have even gone as far to wear #TEAMOCTOPUS T-shirts, to signify their pledge to:

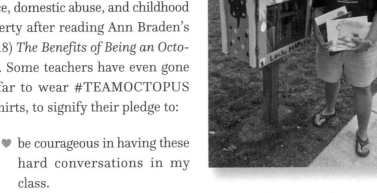

- ♥ be courageous in having these hard conversations in my class.

- ♥ recognize the strengths of all students in my classroom.

- ♥ practice thinking about how systems impact my life and the lives of my students.

- ♥ support impacted students individually and when they are organizing for change.

- ♥ use whatever power I have to change harmful practices and policies within their schools and communities. (Braden 2018)

This idea of being moved to take action speaks to a larger sense of inspiration.

From the Brain to the Heart

If you key the word *inspire* into an online thesaurus, you'll see that each result is connected to the idea of action. That is what inspiration does for us. It propels us forward. We are changed for the better. It ties us to each other with universal desire to somehow make our world a better place. To thrive in the way that Maya Angelou (2015) once wrote: "My mission in life is not merely to survive, but to thrive; and to do so with some passion, some compassion, some humor, and some style."

#StoryIs

"Story is transformative. Healing. Inspiring. Powerful. We each have a unique story only we can tell. That's a powerful thing we should all celebrate."

DARLENE BECK JACOBSON, AUTHOR OF *WISHES, DARES,* AND *HOW TO STAND UP TO A BULLY*

Although in our hearts all of this seems intuitive, research supports plenty of evidence to encourage story as inspiration. In the article "Why Inspiration Matters," Dr. Scott Barry Kaufman (2011) notes how being inspired invites us to take more risks, jump-starts our creativity, and increases our well-being. In the article, he shares how psychologists Todd M. Thrash and Andrew J. Ellio created an "Inspiration Scale," which another study utilized to show that positivity itself is inspirational. Positive experiences elevate our perceptions of self, our desire to pursue goals, and our overall attitude of appreciation. Think about how this concept can be applied to the modeling we do in our classrooms and libraries. The positive experiences we have while reading can inspire us to grow, to change, and to evolve.

Noted scientist, author, and public speaker Dr. Paul J. Zak has done extensive studies on oxytocin, a neurochemical in our brains. In the article "Why Inspiring Stories Make Us React: The Neuroscience of Narrative" (2015), he summarizes a variety of studies—all pointing to how stories trigger inspiration through attentive engagement, transportation, and action. When we're emotionally captivated by a story, we're transported into the characters' narratives. The oxytocin in our brains is associated with concerns for them. Zak explains, "If you pay attention to the story and become emotionally engaged with the story's characters, then it is as if you have been transported into the story's world." This is why many return to *Charlotte's Web* (White 1952) throughout their lives for comfort and inspiration, why you might ask yourself how one of your favorite characters might react or respond if they found themselves in a situation like the one you're currently in, and ultimately why *The One and Only Ivan* (Applegate 2012) spoke to my heart the way it did all those years ago. When we're transported into engaging narratives, our brains are wired to react in a positive way, sparking creativity, making us more empathetic, and increasing our well-being. In fact, this holds true whether the story is happy or sad—a good story will serve to inspire.

Recently, my colleague and friend Margie Myers-Culver, a dedicated and innovative teacher-librarian for thirty-four years, and I made connections to this as we chatted about *story as inspiration*, and she shared something that continued to resonate deep inside my brain. "Every person who's thrown a pebble into a puddle knows what happens. A series of rings radiates from the spot where the stone landed. The distance they travel is determined by a variety of factors, but one truth remains: if the puddle receives no pebble, there will be no ripples." We went on to discuss the importance of how we can be the pebbles in our schools, spreading ripples for the love of reading. If you think of the pebble as inspiration, imagine how many ripples will radiate and multiply. Imagine how long those ripples will spread in the hearts of young readers and writers we work with every day.

Voices From

THE LIBRARIAN'S DESK

Demonstrations of inspiration are as varied as the people who supply them. We all have a story, made from many stories. Successful authors know this, and one of the ways we can take advantage of the connections they help us make through story is to invite them into our communities (either in person or virtually) to talk more about their work and what inspires them. Donna Kouri, a teacher-librarian in Illinois, knows firsthand the power of author visits to inspire students in a variety of ways.

Donna Kouri

Author visits are a tremendous source of joy, inspiration, and celebration. Author visits inspire students to explore literature they might not otherwise have selected. When Kevin Henkes came to share his gentle picture book Waiting (2015), students prepared for his visit by exploring the world of Wemberly in Wemberly Worried (2000), giggling at Lilly's sense of style in Lilly's Purple Plastic Purse (1996), and cheering for Billy Miller as he navigates second grade in The Year of Billy Miller (2013). Their love of Kevin Henkes continued past his visit, as children checked out his many books over and over and over. Had I merely encouraged them to read a book by Kevin Henkes, chances are that wouldn't have happened. But because they felt connected to him after his visit, it did.

This type of inspiration goes beyond the groups that get to see visiting authors. Students talk about the visit with their friends and see the bulletin boards and decorations that line the hallway. Others in the school see the excitement that erupts the day of the visit, and suddenly students who didn't even attend the author's presentation are checking out their books, too. They want to be part of the excitement. Hold lists become long, and family members tell of children bringing newly signed books to dinner and clutching them as they sleep. The energy generated by an author visit lingers long after the visit has ended. Even months later children will eagerly check out a book by one of our previous literary guests.

Author visits also serve as a portal into parts of our world with which students may not be familiar. When Thanhhà Lai visited for her book Listen, Slowly (2016), our students had limited knowledge of Vietnam. But as they became familiar with Vietnam, not only were they able to understand Mai's story, they also understood Thanhhà better as she spoke to them about creating Mai's story. During his visit, when Henry Winkler shared his struggles in school, students learned that the difficulties they have now do not define them and that with perseverance and determination dreams can come true.

Sharing stories with each other, and with our visiting authors and illustrators, makes our hearts grow. We connect to each other as we learn how we are similar, and we grow together as we look into worlds different than our own. We are changed and in the process brought closer together. Visits by authors and illustrators are an inspirational medium that allow this to happen.

In addition to inspiring student interest in authors' and illustrators' work and the world around them, students often leave a guest visit inspired to write and share their own stories. They connect with the author on a personal level. Here, teacher-librarian Rhonda Jenkins expands on Donna's thoughts to further explore the ways our time with authors and illustrators can build personal connections—and through those interactions, lead to even more reading, writing, and deeper levels of inspiration.

Rhonda Jenkins

When I think of how author visits can inspire students, Luke Flowers' visit to my school library immediately comes to mind. We love his Moby Shinobi books, so my students were so excited that he was coming to visit. If there's something that hypes up the excitement, it's decorating the school for the visit. Decorations on the marquee outside, on the display TV in our foyer, on the wall in

the hallway, and a bulletin board dedicated to him and his books! We also had a life-size replica of Moby on the wall in the library!

When the time arrived for his visit, we all became ninjas—a blue T-shirt tied over our heads to resemble a ninja and a Hi-Yah! welcomed him to our school.

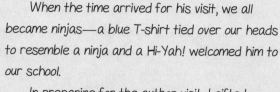

In preparing for the author visit, I gifted copies of Moby Shinobi to each classroom so those who had not yet read one could become familiar. This created a huge desire to check them out from the library! Twenty-five copies only touched the surface of a demand for the books that lasted practically to the end of the school year!

I believe the biggest impact comes when students understand that authors are regular people! Seeing their faces as Luke Flowers spoke to them through his hand puppet warmed my heart. Him teaching them how to draw was truly inspiring. As so many of my students did, one child in particular wrote a book about Moby in his very own style. His name is also Luke! This student drew pictures and asked me to mail them to Luke. I told him I'd do one better and send it out on Twitter. I shared Luke's response with him and he was over-the-moon happy! This connection grew. Luke's mother also thanked Luke Flowers through Twitter. Luke, the author, responded by sending books to the family to complete Luke, the student's, home collection! Two Lukes, friends forever, all because of an author visit!

In person, authors have an amazing ability to bring the stories they write to life. This fosters a greater appreciation for reading and connecting, helping students realize it can be possible for them to write great books too.

From the Heart to the Classroom

Beyond inviting authors into our learning communities, there are many other ways we can create conditions that encourage connections for students' minds, hearts, and interests. As you continue to look for ways to share your own love of story with your students, keep a look out for practices, like the ones included below, that will help you inspire readers with books, authors, and experiences that speak to their hearts.

Booktalking

I love talking about books I feel passionately about. I can trace my love for booktalking all the way back to 1988 when I was a student in Mrs. Villender's second-grade class. I don't believe she ever used the term, but she taught me about the art of *booktalking*—she modeled what a passionate booktalker looked like. Her method was simple. She just talked about books she loved and shared her excitement for them and then invited us to do the same. When we each got to sign up to booktalk one of our favorites, I was hooked.

After spending half my life sharing books this way, you can imagine how excited I was when I joined the Scholastic Book Fairs team and met Alan Boyko—a true champion for booktalking—for the first time. The first questions out of his mouth are always, "What are you reading now?" and "What books are you loving?" During his thirty-one years at Scholastic Book Fairs, he started every meeting with a booktalk, and this practice quickly spread across the company. It became the expectation.

Imagine if this was the expectation in our schools. Imagine if every school day and every faculty meeting started with a booktalk. Imagine if every person on a campus talked about the books that touched their hearts. Imagine how many more students would be inspired to read and share books. If we booktalk every day, we're exposing our students to at least 180 new titles during a school year. Donalyn Miller (2014) often says, "If we want kids to find themselves as readers, value each other, and take risks—both in reading and in life, we must bless their books—and them." When we share our enthusiasm for books and reading, it will rub off on our students. As we all know, word of mouth is extremely effective, and you'll see how much your students appreciate recommendations, especially from peers.

As Dr. Sylvia M. Vardell (2019), professor in the School of Library and Information Studies at Texas Woman's University, notes, "An added bonus is the relationship you develop with children through booktalks and conversations about books. They come to view you as someone who cares about reading and cares about them—something no computer can communicate" (182). In my former district, Family Visitation Day took place once a year. Students were shadowed by family members for the entire school day. As a teacher-librarian, it was a wonderful opportunity to model for family members how to deliver a booktalk and to show how booktalking often inspires students to read more. A quizzical father came over to me after the booktalking session to share that now he understands why his son comes home talking about books and why his son is always asking him to order books with long hold lists. After sharing the booktalk experience firsthand with his son, he found himself more supportive of all the books his son wanted to buy and read. When we connect with students through booktalks, we send ripples of inspiration through our entire communities.

Book Trailers

As a natural extension to booktalking, sharing book trailers with readers can be just as inspiring. I founded my blog, *Watch. Connect. Read.*, because I observed how my students connected with book trailers and author interviews. I wanted a central place to showcase book-related videos and inspire fellow educators to incorporate media in their booktalks and lessons. I include book trailers in almost every booktalking session I give. You can always tell a book trailer resonates with your students when:

1. Students applaud at the end of the trailer.

2. Students run to the catalog to place a hold on the book.

3. Several students ask to watch it again.

By the time my students were in fifth grade, they had viewed hundreds of book trailers and were always excited to explore more. You can find some great examples of book trailers from my students' favorites listed in Figure 3.1.

BOOK TITLE:
The One and Only Bob

AUTHOR: Katherine Applegate

BOOK TITLE:
Our Friend Hedgehog:
The Story of Us

AUTHOR AND ILLUSTRATOR:
Lauren Castillo

BOOK TITLE:
The Little Butterfly That Could

AUTHOR AND ILLUSTRATOR:
Ross Burach

BOOK TITLE:
I Am Every Good Thing

AUTHOR: Derrick Barnes
ILLUSTRATOR: Gordon C. James

BOOK
Bubble Kisses

AUTHOR: Vanessa Williams
ILLUSTRATOR: Tara Nicole Whitaker

FIGURE 3.1 Book Trailers That Inspire Students to Read

For more book trailers, check out the regularly updated Watch. Connect. Read. *posts on my blog at MrSchuReads.com.*

Book Title:
The Adventure Is Now

Author: Jess Redman

Book Title:
Keep It Together, Keiko Carter

Author: Debbi Michiko Florence

Book Title:
My Best Friend

Author: Julie Fogliano
Illustrator: Jillian Tamaki

Book Title:
Lift

Author: Minh Lê
Illustrator: Dan Santat

Book
Allergic

Author: Megan Wagner Lloyd
Illustrator: Michelle Mee Nutter

Book Title:
A Piglet Named Mercy

Author: Kate DiCamillo
Illustrator: Chris Van Dusen

Author or Illustrator Visits

Author visits can bring an entire class, an entire school, an entire community together through story. Connecting with a children's book creator through an in-person visit or a virtual visit is one way to bring joy and a spoonful of inspiration directly into a school. In our former school library, my students and I hosted thirty-seven in-person visits and at least 100 virtual visits. One of my favorite activities the day after an author or an illustrator visited our school library was when students wrote anonymous comments on strips of paper about what they gleaned from the visit. Here are four comments from when Newbery Medalist Sharon Creech visited our library. Notice how frequently the idea of inspiration shines through these children's comments.

- ♥ "Sharon Creech has inspired me to become an author."

- ♥ "Your books inspire . . . your writing is my heart's desire. All I want to say . . . is that your visit made my day."

- ♥ "I never used to visualize when I was reading, so I did not always read books. Sharon Creech's (2003) *Granny Torrelli Makes Soup* taught me to visualize when I read books. Sharon inspired me."

- ♥ "I loved her inspiring presentation. We were planning for her visit for weeks. We were on the edge of our seats waiting to meet her. I like how she changes her voice when she reads."

Children carry these visits in their hearts often for the rest of their lives. And with a little intentional planning we can make them even more successful and, in that way, more inspirational. Through the years I have collected a handful of tips that will help you create a more meaningful guest visit for everyone involved.

You don't have to be Ina Garten to host a successful author or illustrator visit; you just have to keep a few simple tips in mind:

1. Tell your students the author or illustrator is visiting your school. That might sound too apparent, but sometimes a guest shows up and nobody on the campus knows about it in advance.

2. One of the ways you can build excitement is by helping your students become experts on the author or illustrator well in advance of their visit. Talk about the guest's craft and style, explore their website, read aloud and share excerpts from the author's work, and experiment with the illustrator's techniques and styles. Share with your students what you love about the guest's work and why you invited them to come.

3. The more students are involved in the preparation, the more inspired they will be during and after the visit. Yes, you can do all of this on your own, but it's much more effective and inspiring when students are involved from the start. As students get to know the author and illustrator and excitement about the visit begins to build, invite them into the work of preparing the campus and the presentation space.

- Ask students to prepare and deliver a welcome speech and a thank-you speech or perform a quick reader's theater to welcome the guest.

- Create posters welcoming the author and illustrator. Decorate the lobby, halls, library, and speaking area based on the theme of a book.

- Coordinate with the art teacher to see if their lessons can incorporate the guest's visit in some way such as creating artwork around the theme of a book or building models of a scene or an artifact from the book to be displayed using items such as clay, Lego bricks, or a 3-D printer.

#StoryIs

"Story is illustrating, is learning, is growing, is empowering, is . . ."

Lauren Castillo, author-illustrator of *Our Friend Hedgehog: The Story of Us*

- Develop writing experiences based on the guest's books. For instance, you might collaboratively write a book to present to the author or illustrator or invite students to design a thank-you of some sort to present to the guest.

4. Don't forget, there are lots of ways you can keep the joy and momentum going after your visit. Consider debriefing your time together by talking about the strengths of the visit, what students enjoyed most, what they got out of it, and what they might do differently next time. As mentioned earlier, inviting students to write thank-you notes is another great way to reflect on your time with an author or illustrator.

CONNECTING WITH AUTHORS AND ILLUSTRATORS WHEN IN-PERSON VISITS AREN'T AN OPTION

Sometimes in-person visits aren't always possible. Perhaps the school's budget for author and illustrator visits is limited. Maybe the guest you'd like to have visit is too busy or too far away to make an in-person appearance. My friend and award-winning author-illustrator Debbie Ridpath Ohi put together a wonderful list of ways to connect with authors and illustrators when they can't come to you. Here, she offers some ideas for making this happen with your reading communities along with some tips for keeping the experience productive.

#StoryIs

"Story is what makes the everyday real. It takes a private thought or a private witness into the public realm, and transforms the everyday into legend."

KEVIN NOBLE MAILLARD, AUTHOR OF *FRY BREAD: A NATIVE AMERICAN FAMILY STORY*

Debbie Ohi

Consider virtual visits through platforms such as Skype. Many writers are happy to connect virtually with readers, and Kate Messner keeps a growing list of authors who Skype with classes and book clubs. Use the QR code provided to link to Kate's website.

Skype is no longer the only option when it comes to virtual author and illustrator visits! I've also recently started to use Zoom, Flipgrid, and Google Meet to talk with young readers, do interactive drawing demos, answer questions, show them sketches, and much more. For everyone to get the most out of these virtual visits and to help things run smoothly, make sure your students are familiar with virtual visit procedures in advance, and consider some of these helpful tips that I've learned through my own experiences as well as from educators:

- Make sure your students are familiar with the visiting creator's work before the visit. Read one or more of their books. If possible, have multiple copies available. Ask them to come up with questions they might like to ask. Look on the creator's website for bonus material and suggested classroom activities related to their books.

- Be sure to test the connection before the visit, using the same setup that you would on the day of the visit and around the same time. Ideally, this can be done with the creator. I strongly recommend using a wired connection rather than wireless to avoid lag. Lag can quickly suck the energy and excitement out of a virtual visit. If I notice lag when I begin a virtual visit, I have to switch from call-and-response interactive mode to pure presentation mode.

- When discussing the day and time of the virtual visit, be sure to specify the time zone. The day before the visit, send a friendly email to the book creator reminding them of all the details, including the time zone.

- Exchange phone numbers with the visiting creator, just in case of technical glitches right before or during the visit.

- If there is a Q&A segment, make sure that the creator is able to clearly hear the question. Ideally, have the student asking a question come up to the laptop (or whatever device is being used), introduce themselves, and ask their question. Show them where to stand and where to look into the webcam while they are asking a question.

- For younger students, I advise having questions prepared and screened in advance; otherwise you may get not-quite-questions like "I know how to draw, too!" and "My hamster's name is Kirby!" Another advantage of having questions prepared and screened ahead of time is avoiding duplicate questions.

- For virtual chat environments like Zoom and Google Meet with multiple participants, know how to mute and unmute students. When the book creator is speaking, you'll want to make sure the students are all muted to avoid background noises interfering. If possible, ask students to leave their webcams on so that the visiting creator can see their faces.

And, finally, Debbie leaves us with an important reminder: "Don't forget the illustrator," she notes, "especially when it comes to picture books and illustrated chapter books. So often I see people reaching out only to the author of an illustrated book. One way to reach an author might be through the illustrator. When educators or parents send me feedback from a young reader about a book I've illustrated, I always try to let the author know as well."

Whose Heart Needs a Copy of This Book?

If you haven't already noticed, the status of hearts are always on my mind. My rule is if I talk about a book during a school visit or during a professional development presentation, I try to give away a copy of the book. I usually hold it up and ask, "Whose heart needs a copy of this book?" I read the room. I look people in the eyes, searching for a heart that is waiting to be inspired by this book. I ask myself which heart truly needs this book.

Recently, during a school visit, I was about to place a copy of Dav Pilkey's (2019) *Dog Man: Fetch-22* into the hands of a second grader, when, across the room, a third grader stood up and shouted out, "Wait! Mr. Schu, my heart needs that book!" I remember thinking, both hearts need this book. Thankfully, I was able to put a copy into both hands—both hearts left the room happy and hopefully inspired to think more about books of their hearts. Tell your students about the books of your heart, those books that will stay with you forever. Share with them the books that changed you, shaped you, inspired you. Invite your students to share the books of their hearts. You don't have to give books away to incorporate this idea. If you want to try for a more concrete connection, consider ways to bring this process into your physical space through displays around your learning community. This could be as simple as creating a bulletin board that showcases each student's favorite book of their heart as shown in Figure 3.2.

Weekend Update

Every child who walks into your classroom or library needs opportunities to tell their stories and find themselves in stories. I recently ran into Ananya, one of my former fourth graders, who is now a senior in college. She reminded me about Weekend Update, one of her favorite memories from the fourth grade, where she was able to share what she was excited about and to learn more about her classmates. Every Monday, we would gather in a circle to share one thing from our weekend. This weekly ritual allowed us to bond as

FIGURE 3.2 Whose Hearts Needs a Copy of This Book? Displays

a learning community and to see each other as individuals beyond the walls of our classroom. Updates ranged from a lost tooth to the birth of a sibling to a book discovered at a local bookshop. I collected these stories of their hearts as a way to match them with books I hoped would inspire them. Learning about their favorite TV shows, music, and the movies they watched multiple times helped bring their experiences into the classroom. There are so many books I would have never booktalked and introduced to students if it were not for Weekend Update. There are so many conversations we may have never had. The more we know what our students love, the better we can match them with the perfect books.

I take notes on almost every book I read. I was especially grateful for this practice when selecting ten books to share with you in this chapter. I looked through all of my notebooks searching for the word *inspire*. Following is a collection of books I believe will motivate you and your students to learn more about Teresa Carreño, to combat climate change, and to draw, paint, plant, dig, dance, read, and more. Happy reading and exploring!

🎨 *Gurple and Preen: A Broken Crayon Cosmic Adventure* by Linda Sue Park; illustrated by Debbie Ridpath Ohi

Inspired by Debbie Ridpath Ohi's Broken Crayon Art series, this is the story of Gurple and Preen, aliens whose ship crashes, breaks apart, and spills its rather unusual contents—CRAYONS! They must rescue the PODS (package of unbroken crayons) before the time is up. Gurple only sees the bad in the situation, whereas Preen uses creativity and ingenuity to harness the broken crayons into just what is needed to save the day.

APPLICATION TO STORY AS INSPIRATION

Debbie Ridpath Ohi's art will likely inspire readers to create their own broken crayon art. Students can unleash their creativity as they use broken crayons as the basis for creations that are limited only by their imagination. Pair this title with Barney Saltzberg's *Beautiful Oops*.

🎨 *Dancing Hands: How Teresa Carreño Played the Piano for President Lincoln* by Margarita Engle; illustrated by Rafael López

Pianist extraordinaire Teresa Carreño had a difficult life as a child, but her music helped her find joy during dark times. At the age of ten, she was invited to play for a grieving Abraham Lincoln and, despite her fears and worries, helped him and his family find joy during a difficult time.

APPLICATION TO STORY AS INSPIRATION

Even though Teresa was nervous about playing for President Lincoln, unsure that the poorly tuned piano would produce beautiful music, she did. The inspirational way she showed courage by not giving into her worry brought joy to Lincoln's family during times of uncertainty.

🎨 *Little Libraries, Big Heroes* by Miranda Paul; illustrated by John Parra

Todd Bol, while grieving the loss of his mother, designed a library outside his home to honor her love of reading. It took a while, but this library became an important part of the community. He wondered if similar libraries could bring joy to communities around the world. With perseverance, determination, and help from family and friends, he turned this single library into a global movement.

APPLICATION TO STORY AS INSPIRATION

Todd started with a small idea, a single library outside his home, but quickly had a vision of similar libraries all over the world. He shared this dream with friends and family and they worked tirelessly to make this happen, not giving up when it seemed difficult. Thanks to this dedication and vision, Little Free Libraries are making the lives of others better across the globe.

🎨 *Our House Is on Fire: Greta Thunberg's Call to Save the Planet* by Jeanette Winter

This is the story of Greta Thunberg's transformation from a quiet, lonely girl to a social activist working to save the climate. It highlights Greta's passion and perseverance in fighting for climate change, her role in the children's movement to halt it, and her transformation to an international speaker on the topic.

Greta is young, yet she has made such a difference and has spurred an international movement. Greta inspires students to see that anyone is capable of starting a movement, even a child. Readers will want to become more like Greta and join her and the many children working to stop climate change.

Titan and the Wild Boars: The True Cave Rescue of the Thai Soccer Team by Susan Hood and Pathana Sornhiran; illustrated by Dow Phumiruk

This story tells the story of a boy, Titan, and his soccer team who were trapped in a cave in Thailand during monsoon season. It describes the difficulties in rescuing the team and breaks down their ordeal day by day as well as the bravery and strength shown not only by the team and their coach but also by the rescuers and parents.

APPLICATION TO STORY AS INSPIRATION

This story inspires readers to have hope. Even under the direst of circumstances, those trapped remained hopeful as did those working to secure their rescue. It inspires us to be brave and trust others, especially those who work so hard to maintain hope even when the situation seems hopeless.

Saturday by Oge Mora

Saturdays are the best day of the week because that is the day that Ava's mother has off work. Saturdays are spectacular days full of fun and this one promises to be full of grand adventures. Unfortunately, Saturday does not turn out at all as planned, but Ava and her mom realize that all is not lost because they have each other.

APPLICATION TO STORY AS INSPIRATION

This story inspires students to look for and be grateful for love. Things may not always go as planned, and sometimes it is easy to get frustrated, but even the worst day can be a great day when we spend it with someone we love.

🌀 *The Important Thing About Margaret Wise Brown* by Mac Barnett; illustrated by Sarah Jacoby

Margaret Wise Brown was the author of many beloved books, including *Goodnight Moon*. This book tells the reader many important things about Margaret Wise Brown, including the fact that not everybody thought her books were good books for children and that an influential librarian tried to keep them off library shelves. But the important thing about Margaret Wise Brown is that she did not give up, and now children all over the world know her books.

APPLICATION TO STORY AS INSPIRATION

This book inspires children to persevere and surprises them with the truth. They may be shocked to learn that a childhood classic was not always accepted and that its author was a little unusual. But in the end, this book that seemed odd is now treasured and its author is revered.

🌀 *Carl and the Meaning of Life* by Deborah Freedman

Carl is a worm who, when asked why he spends his time digging through the dirt, is unsure. He goes on a journey to find the answer to this question and comes up empty-handed until he realizes that by stopping his digging, the ground has become hard, which makes life difficult for many creatures. Carl learns his role in their lives and how, without him, their lives aren't the same.

APPLICATION TO STORY AS INSPIRATION

This story shows the importance of each individual and how their presence impacts others. Even when we feel small and insignificant, we are important to the world and in the lives of others.

 *Bear Came Along* by Richard T. Morris; illustrated by LeUyen Pham

This tells the story of a river and a number of animals. Each does not realize something until they encounter the next animal or obstacle. Together, they learn that although they each thought they were living their life alone, they weren't.

APPLICATION TO STORY AS INSPIRATION

This story shows how we are all connected. We may think we are living a solitary life, but we aren't. It shows us the community we are all part of, how we keep each other going, and how sometimes it takes one seemingly insignificant event to make us realize this.

Sam & Eva by Debbie Ridpath Ohi

Sam is happily drawing on a wall when Eva comes by and, to his surprise, adds to his drawing. Sam is initially not pleased, but what ensues is collaborative art at its best as two friends draw together, eventually finding a common story.

APPLICATION TO STORY AS INSPIRATION

Sam and Eva will inspire readers to collaborate and work together to create a story through drawings. Readers witness how making art can be a shared experience and will likely feel inspired to try to draw and create a story in the same way Sam and Eva did.

My favorite titles for story as inspiration

Story as Clarifier

What comes to mind when you think about the idea of clarity? Do you think about topics that you want to understand better? Do you think about times when something became clearer to you? Do you think about misunderstandings you've had about yourself and others? Do you think about an unexpected aha moment that smacks you across the head and wakes you up? When we consider story as clarifier, all of these things play a role.

More to the point, can you recall a book that:

- ♥ taught you more about something you were interested in?

- ♥ clarified a confusion you had about a topic?

- ♥ taught you something new you weren't expecting?

- ♥ helped you better understand something about yourself?

- ♥ invited you to see a situation or another person differently?

- ♥ challenged a deeply held belief?

- ♥ highlighted your awareness and increased empathy?

- ♥ helped you rethink a misconception?

- ♥ affirmed something you already felt was true in your heart?

Maybe it was during your dinosaur phase in the second grade, or perhaps it was when you were feeling alone as a teenager, or maybe even during your adult life when you had a realization that made you question and unlearn something. Mary comes to mind when I think about story as clarifier. I was lucky enough to be her third-grade teacher and then her teacher-librarian later when she was in the fifth grade. Mary was always building things, designing imaginary worlds, checking out nonfiction books about a wide range of topics, and decorating her desk—inside and out—with handmade and store-bought tchotchkes. When she became interested in a new topic, she would read every book on the subject. She wanted to become an expert. Her enthusiasm for the topics she felt passionately about inspired her classmates. They inspired me. I still refer to it as the Mary effect. For example, she created a club to teach her classmates about all things Webkinz, facilitated a hands-on workshop about the art of folding origami, and even started a nonfiction book club that met during recess. She inspired her peers to dig deep, to seek clarity about what they were interested in and passionate about.

I was similar to Mary as a child. If I became interested in a topic or put my mind to something, I went all in. It consumed me. I asked tons of questions. I researched. In the second grade, I checked out and read every book about planets from the public library, bought spaced-themed

#StoryIs

"Story is essential to life. Without storytelling we would probably not have survived as humans. We need stories to teach us about the past, and to share traditions with each other, and even sometimes predict the future. It's such a powerful tool, which is why I'm a writer."

Saadia Faruqi, author of *Yusuf Azeem Is Not a Hero*

bulletin board kits from the teachers' store to decorate my bedroom (or my classroom as I referred to it), and *forced* my imaginary students to sit through a myriad of lessons filled with fun facts and interesting tidbits about our solar system. In the fourth grade, I fell in love with musical theater. Songs and scores danced around inside my heart. I'm almost certain I rented every movie musical in the local video store's collection, checked out original cast recordings of Broadway musicals from the public library, and browsed the stacks looking for books about *Little Shop of Horrors*, *La Cage aux Folles*, *The Sound of Music*, Jennifer Holliday, Alan Meinken, Jerry Herman, and Annette Funicello. I wanted to learn everything I could about Broadway musicals and composers. If only YouTube had been around back then.

In the seventh grade, my grandma, who was my best friend and the person who understood me the best, was diagnosed with pancreatic cancer. It felt as though the floor collapsed beneath my feet. I spent many afternoons at the public library researching and clarifying complicated questions about pancreatic cancer, the Whipple procedure, and acute respiratory distress syndrome. I think it was a healthy and productive way to understand and try to accept what she was going through. I needed facts. It helped me process her cancer.

At the same time, I was struggling with anxiety, low feelings of self-worth, and disordered eating. I felt alone, confused, and consumed with questions about what I was thinking and feeling. One afternoon, I found the most isolated computer terminal in the public library. I typed the keywords *anorexia, bulimia, Tracey Gold,* and *eating disorders* into the library's catalog. The results led me to articles and feature stories in magazines such as *People* and *Entertainment Weekly*. It led me to the microfiche machine where I read scholarly articles filled with words and concepts I didn't understand. It led me to Afterschool Specials and Karen Carpenter. Eventually, I found my way to other books and genres—some more helpful than others—and even though I wouldn't fully admit it to myself or publicly for at least two more years, my research helped clarify that I had an eating disorder.

Years later, and thanks to some wonderful therapists and specialists, it's mostly behind me now, but I still think about how seeing myself in those stories saved my life—and, essentially, my heart. Perhaps you had similar experiences of your own where you'd clandestinely escape to the library to clarify questions such as divorce, sexuality, racism, war, and other topics pressing on your heart. You found clarification through research. Maybe you found comfort and a better understanding of the world and yourself.

There are multiple layers to this idea of story as clarifier, and different stories will push you in different directions. At its heart, clarifying is about perspective—refining and expanding the way we see ourselves, others, and our world. Our thinking around this topic may naturally bring to mind nonfiction topics and texts, but fiction texts have a place and a lot to offer here as well. In this chapter, we'll look at different ways story can act as a clarifier for us and our learning communities.

From the Brain to the Heart

On its most obvious level, story is a way into research and inquiry. As a classroom teacher, teacher-librarian, and, now, university instructor, story and inquiry-based instruction are at the heart of many of the learning experiences I've invited students into. Dr. Mihaly Csikszentmihaly introduced the idea of flow to many of us and explains it as "A state in which people are so involved in an activity that nothing else seems to matter" (Csikszentmihalyi 1990, 4). After teaching this concept to my elementary school students, it wasn't

#StoryIs

"Story is life. Every word, every paragraph, and every turn of the page gives us new meaning to life."

ALICIA D. WILLIAMS, AUTHOR OF *SHIRLEY CHISHOLM DARED*

unusual for one of them to bring up this concept in the middle of a project to describe that all-too-common feeling of being lost in a book. If you've ever been in the I-can't-put-this-book-down mode, you've experienced flow.

In fact, allowing students the choice-driven option to get lost in inquiry sets them up to be in this state of flow (Borovay et al. 2019)—in other words, to get lost in a book. As students work through their innermost curiosities, as they check out twenty books on dinosaurs, as they explore every dog breed, as they research all the places they'll travel when they grow up, they experience what it's like to be a real reader, to lose themselves through story as they clarify their understandings about various concepts that speak directly to their hearts. This is something we want for every reader.

When we take a moment to look deeper, stories can invite us to clarify who we are, our understandings of the world, and the misconceptions we may not have even known we held. As I write this chapter, the idea of story as clarifier is naturally on my mind. I try different ways of slipping it into conversations. If we were together in person, I would ask you to share what story as clarifier means to you. I would invite you to share the stories that helped you better understand yourself and the world. Recently, during a virtual book club meeting, I asked everyone to share a book that comes to mind when they think about the idea of story as clarifier.

One colleague shared how Sherri L. Smith's (2020) *The Blossom and the Firefly* clarified misconceptions about their understanding of Japanese culture and mindset before, during, and after World War II. This young adult novel is told in two voices. We hear from Hanna,

#StoryIs

"Stories are full experiences in themselves, especially the ones we connect to the most. I had a writing teacher who said that in drawing from our own experiences, we should also use our reading experiences. They are also part of what shapes us. I always remembered that and have looked at stories a bit differently since."

VEERA HIRANANDANI, AUTHOR OF *THE NIGHT DIARY*

a member of the Nadeshiko Unit girls of Chiran Junior High School in Chiran, Japan, and Taro, a pilot who volunteers to be a part of the kamikaze attacks. This story helped to broaden their viewpoint of Japanese youths' commitment to honor their country, their communities, and their parents. It solidifies the importance of investigating and presenting history from multiple viewpoints.

Another colleague brought up Silas Wade, the main character in Phil Bildner's (2020) middle-grade novel, *A High Five for Glenn Burke*. Silas knows he's gay, but he's struggling to fully admit it to himself and others. After extensively researching Glenn Burke, a gay Major League baseball player in the 1970s, he starts to better understand himself. He often imagines what Glenn Burke would have felt or done in a situation. He feels a connection to him. "I was thinking about Glenn Burke. I'm still thinking about Glenn Burke. No wonder he was never able to play as well as people thought he would. No wonder he kept getting hurt. All this stuff weighs you down and holds you down and keeps you down. And it weighs you down and holds you down and keeps you down more and more and more with every passing

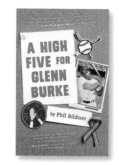

moment" (Bildner 172). By applying aspects of Glenn Burke's story to himself, he is able to tell his own truth. In turn, Glenn's and Silas's stories can help readers clarify their own stories.

Another colleague shared how she stopped reading *A High Five for Glenn Burke* several times not only to ponder over the words but to reflect on the thousands of students who entered and left her school library over the years. Did she treat them all equally, welcoming them with warmth, insight, and openness? Did the materials selected and lessons taught reflect all types of readers and learners? Were there students like Silas who she might have overlooked? She reminded me of how important it is for all students to have access to stories like *A High Five for Glenn Burke*. In a guest post on teacher-librarian and author Travis Jonker's blog, Phil Bildner (2020) writes, "*A High Five for Glenn Burke* is the book I wish I had when I was twelve. Middle school me didn't know there were others like me. Middle school me felt all alone in the world. Middle school me certainly didn't know queer kids played sports. A book like this would have given me hope."

In their article titled "Stories of Power and the Power of Stories," Dr. Andrew Green and Simon Bradford (2011) expand this concept and remind us that "stories are currency and capital—the stuff of social interaction; our interface with the world; our way of reading and writing our experiences as human beings, whether literally with pen and paper or figuratively." This is the power stories can have as we invite and allow students to follow their hearts' curiosities and get lost in texts that affirm and challenge their perspectives.

Voices From

THE TEACHER'S DESK

As we think about bringing the idea of story as clarifier into the classroom in a concrete way, I'm reminded of the work of my fifth-grade teaching friends Dr. Karen Biggs-Tucker and Dr. Brian Tucker, who find creative ways to invite inquiry in their literacy workshops and make room for students to experience story as they chase down their curiosities.

Karen and Brian

The day is getting ready to start, and we are waiting outside of our classroom doors that are right across the hall from each other (yes, married colleagues being "grade-level neighbors" has its advantages and challenges). As our students come up the stairs, through the hallway, and into our rooms, we hear the conversations of the fifth graders that we look forward to spending our time learning alongside.

They talk about their weekends, their friends, and their families, but they also wonder about themselves, their worlds, and what is going to happen in their futures.

Our day always begins with a book. On this particular day, we begin with A Place Inside of Me: A Poem to Heal the Heart by Zetta Elliott and Noa Denmon (2020). In this book, a young African American boy shares the feelings that he experiences in life as he navigates the world being Black. As we notice the feelings, emotions, and thoughts of the main character, students wonder about why the world is experienced differently for young people of different races. "Why aren't all kids treated the same?" asks Maggie as she looks at the pages and talks with the peers around her. Another student wonders, "What can we do when we see someone treated unfairly?" As the conversation continues, the wonderings grow and evolve as students struggle with the big questions that they see not only in their daily lives but in the world around them. As we finish reading the book, we begin writing about our thinking and then look for other books that will help continue the conversation about understanding our feelings about race and equity and how they impact how we live in the world.

As we move into our literacy workshop time, learners make choices about their reading and writing based on the goals that they have for themselves as learners. Often students have questions about their world that they want to answer through their reading and writing. Research provides an opportunity for them to explore what they are wondering about in the world around them. Whether they have a passion for music, history, or animals, the workshop provides a place for them to research, learn, and create artifacts to share what they have learned with others. Their questions provide the motivation for learning and sharing that learning with others. We know that is what lifelong learners do, and creating spaces for them to practice doing that is a priority for us in our classrooms. Sitting alongside them during this time provides some of our favorite times as we leverage the conversations that we have with students to help them grow as literacy learners and build relationships with them as individuals. Hearing them talk about their passions and wonders helps us learn about who they are and what they care about and helps guide us in how we can support them as they grow as human beings in our learning spaces.

Creating spaces for students to explore their questions through inquiry allows them to research and learn about the topics that interest them; because of the relationships that we have established with them, we also have the opportunity to guide their thinking to explore ideas that will extend them beyond the four walls of the classroom. As more students begin to understand and ask questions about issues related to climate change, social justice, and making the world a better place, we have the opportunity to create citizens of a world that will change for the better. When a student asks the question, "Why aren't all people treated equally?" it creates an opportunity not only to explore issues related to racial equity and social justice, but also to think about how students can become allies to their classmates who might be victims of racism. When a student wonders, "How can I recycle and make the world greener?" it allows a space to discuss climate change and student leaders like Greta Thunberg who are actively working to make change at a young age. We can—through the reading, writing, and conversations that we have with our students—empower them to speak up and become agents for change, making our world a better place for future generations.

At the end of the day, we take a moment to have students reflect on the questions they have asked, the learning they have done, and the wondering they have already created as a way to prepare for tomorrow. As we celebrate the day, we look ahead to tomorrow. What learning will await us? What questions will we have? How will we look for the answers to them? How will our questions help us grow as learners and humans? As we watch our students pack up and walk out the door, we are reminded that the world is in good hands as long as they keep wondering, questioning, and searching . . . because in the curiosity of this generation, there is hope for our future.

From the Heart to the Classroom

Although readers take naturally to chasing curiosities through the reading experience, there are specific things we can do to encourage them to seek clarity through research and story. This includes practical activities as well conditions we can establish and maintain to help readers get lost in story and inquiry. Through these processes, we create an environment in which curiosity is not only allowed and encouraged but also honored, which helps make for a more meaningful experience for students.

Wondering Together

In *Unleashing Student Superpowers*, Hadley J. Ferguson and Kristen Swanson (2014) refer to *wondering* as a superpower. Indeed! I always encourage students to wonder and to ask a lot of questions—questions about the world, about themselves, about those around them, about the things they would like to create and change, about big things and small things, about serious things and funny things. Regular activities like *question of the day* where you simply explore a thought-provoking inquiry, *wonder walls* where students post their burning questions, and even daily visits to *Wonderopolis.org* where "the wonders of learning never cease" keep students in the practice of asking questions and primes their pumps for future curiosity-driven reading. It's not unusual for a question of the day or a Wonderopolis post to spur a community into a weeklong investigative spree with students reading everything they can get their hands on to learn more. When classrooms share wondering experiences like this together, reading as a response to curiosity becomes a more instinctive part of what readers naturally do.

If you've never had a chance to visit Wonderopolis.org, you'll find tons of thought-provoking questions such as "How do you know a source is valid?," "Who invented kindergarten?," and "What is a rhombicosidodecahedron?"

#StoryIs

"Story is where we discover ourselves, our voice, and our strength. It is where we learn we are not alone."

Elly Swartz, author of Dear Student

Genius Hour

I always knew it was Genius Hour when fourth graders came running into the library with big, bright smiles. They were always so excited, so eager, to dive into a self-selected project. I saw different aspects of their personalities and lives in those moments. As I got to know their interests and curiosities, I felt more confident in my ability to match them with books, especially nonfiction texts.

There are a variety of ways you can establish your own Genius Hour, and you'll find lots of ideas online. But at its heart, Genius Hour is a time you set aside for students to research a burning question about a topic in a way that makes the most sense to them. For example, teacher-librarian Donna Kouri shared with me about the time her students wanted to create video games during Genius Hour. She introduced them to Bloxels, a "simple yet powerful way to create characters, art, and stories to share with the world" (edu. bloxelsbuilder.com). They learned about pixelation and how it's used to create scenes. They researched games that used pixelation and ultimately created their own video game. The students readily admitted they didn't know what they were doing at first, but they weren't afraid to research, experiment, and learn from their mistakes. By creating the video game, they also engaged in the art of story. They had to determine the goal of the game, who the characters were, what problems they would encounter, and how they could overcome these problems. Through their project, they became storytellers in a way that was likely more engaging to them than writing it down on paper.

This open-ended nature and evolving thinking inherent in Genius Hour allows students to learn about anything they want, to conduct self-guided research, and to present their findings to their peers. As Elizabeth Barrera Rush (2017) writes in *Bringing Genius Hour to Your Library*, "Time in school to pursue a Genius Hour project draws the outside world into the world of academics and conveys the message that these worlds are not mutually exclusive" (3). I would argue even further that Genius Hour is a perfect time to encourage inquiry learning and for readers to seek clarity about a topic. It's an opportunity for students to explore their passions and to spend time focusing on what they really love. For many, it is their chance to shine.

Makerspaces

Makerspaces have become a common feature in many libraries today. Like Genius Hour, makerspaces allow students to pursue their interests and embed academic skills in the process. However, in a makerspace, the student is put in the role of creator. They're thinking outside of the box as they wonder and problem solve, without the expectation that their activity is tied to research and presentation. They're creating for the pure joy of it. They're trying something new and revising it when it doesn't work. They're learning to persevere and to wonder. You can almost feel a sense of flow at work as students make, tinker, create, and build. That is the heart of the makerspace. It mirrors what we do as readers when we're lost in a clarifying experience.

#StoryIs

"Story is discovery. Stories open up worlds for us to grow into. They give us the capacity to experience new lives and different perspectives. One of the most powerful things about story is that it allows us to step outside of ourselves and see others and ourselves with new understanding. I love that."

LINDSAY LACKEY, AUTHOR OF *ALL THE IMPOSSIBLE THINGS*

What I admire about makerspaces is that activities lead students to stories and stories lead them to activities. It is a place where they can explore some of their heart's deepest wonderings. Oftentimes when students discover an activity they enjoy, they want to learn how to take it further, and—in this process—they have many opportunities to make connections to stories. Books, both fiction and nonfiction, are key components of any makerspace. Makers learn to craft basic bracelets using Rainbow Loom and then check out a Rainbow Loom activity

book to take their creativity even further. Students who love online gaming come to the library seeking Tracey Baptiste's (2018) *Minecraft: The Crash* and apply what they learn from the book as they start building complex items using a 3D printer. Students who are big fans of Varian Johnson and Shannon Wright's *Twins* (2020), Raina Telgemeier's (2019) *Guts*, or Jerry Craft's (2020) *Class Act* come to the makerspace to draw. They seek out books such as *Adventures in Cartooning* (Strum, Arnold, and Frederick-Frost 2009) or how-to-draw books by Ed Emberly as they explore creating their own comic strips or graphic novels.

Makerspaces are an essential part of a school library because they intimately connect a student's passion to literature. These passions that grow from their tinkering often drive them into an investigative stance to learn more about a topic or how to accomplish a goal. Books, websites, and how-to videos are the means to ignite students' pursuits; they are a natural way for students to clarify the interests they have.

Conditions for Curiosity

It's no secret the best teaching happens when we set conditions and let students drive the learning. In *Cultivating Curiosity in K–12 Classrooms*, Dr. Wendy L. Ostroff (2016) asserts, "Co-creating a curiosity classroom requires some degree of humility. Teachers have to cease being in charge and listen to the multitude of voices in the classroom with equal respect" (8). You don't have to set up a makerspace or hold a Genius Hour for inquiry and self-discovery to be woven into the fiber

#StoryIs

"Story is how we make sense of life, of the world, and of ourselves. It's how humans keep from getting lost in a chaos of time-fragments!"

SALLY J. PLA, AUTHOR OF *BENJI, THE BAD DAY, AND ME*

of your learning community. This is often done through modeling and the examples we set from our own curiosity. Allow your students to see you as a human being by sharing with them the passions you like to pursue. Explore inquiry together and honor individual journeys through story. Here, we are not talking about things we do, but ways we are as learners. Honor the time it takes to get lost in a quest. It isn't a worksheet. It isn't an activity. It's a way of being.

This could be as simple as embedding curiosity and student-centered inquiry into everyday practices like independent reading and conferring with students. On her blog *Crawling out of the Classroom*, fifth-grade teacher Jess Lifshitz regularly shares how she embeds inquiry into lessons. I've returned many times to an incredibly powerful blog post she wrote in 2019, especially these words: "When my students are really resistant to something I am asking them to do in the classroom, if I stop and reflect on why, it is almost always because they are too far from the center of the work. What I am asking them to do is not meaningful to them; it does not feel driven by their own thoughts and curiosity. In short, I usually need to find a way to weave more inquiry into the work. In my mind, inquiry is the closest that I have ever come, in my classroom, to mimicking the natural desire to learn that so freely exists in my students when they are outside of the classroom."

In addition to keeping curiosity-driven practices at the heart of our teaching, Stephanie Harvey and Annie Ward (2017) encourage us to consider practical actions we can take to cultivate conditions of curiosity in our classrooms and libraries, such as making our wondering visible by regularly modeling our curiosity, honoring students' questioning more than their knowing, and making time for students to follow their hearts' interests through investigation.

Beyond modeling curiosity and implementing inquiry-driven activities, the authors of *From Curiosity to Deep Learning* (Coiro, Dobler, and Pelekis 2019) remind us that in the end, it's best when we set the conditions and trust students to lead the way, writing, "The positive ways that students interact with teachers and with each other lay the foundation for building a culture where learning is valued. Children can begin to feel empowered and confident in their growing ability to control their own learning decisions with support from their peers. In addition, time spent developing personal connections with individual students supports growth in their identity as a valued member in their classroom learning community" (36).

Mr. Schu Suggests

Again, when we consider story as clarifier, often our most impactful actions are to simply encourage students to pursue their interests as we connect them with stories that will enhance their journey. Here, I've highlighted ten book titles that you might share to encourage, model, and honor inquiry and self-discovery. In this list, you will encounter characters who ask big and important questions, a family and friends making fry bread, inspirational biographies, a unique look at the life of a bee, and more.

🌀 *Fry Bread: A Native American Family Story* by Kevin Noble Maillard; illustrated by Juana Martinez-Neal

This is the lyrical story of family and friends making fry bread, a recipe imbued with comfort, community, and tradition. Fry bread is food, shape, sound, color, flavor, time, art, history, place, and nation. Kevin Noble Maillard, an enrolled citizen of the Seminole Nation, includes an eight-page note in the back matter that explains the history of fry bread and the honest history of Native Americans and their treatment and that dispels misconceptions of Indigenous people. As Kevin shared when I interviewed him, "I hope *Fry Bread* becomes a go-to book about inclusion and equality. As much as it showcases food and family, it also emphasizes the value of diversity. There are so many ways to make fry bread, which comes in all shapes, sizes, and colors. The way I was taught to make it is fairly different from the fry bread made by most Native families. I think that this celebration of different flavors and forms of fry bread, which is so central to Indian culture, is also a love lyric for all of the different shapes and colors of Native people in America. Each form is valid and 'authentic,' without one being more legitimate than the other" (Maillard 2019). Make sure you spend time poring over the endpapers; they name and honor Indigenous nations and communities currently within the United States.

APPLICATION TO STORY AS CLARIFIER

Fry Bread shares the history of Native Americans, which is often overlooked and mistaught in schools. It dispels some commonly held misconceptions. The story can be especially resonant with Native readers who will see elements of their tribal nations celebrated. One of my graduate students shared about a time when she read *Fry Bread* to her students. "One student," she wrote me, "who usually listens and doesn't participate much in conversations, upon realizing that *Fry Bread* was about him, stood next to me with his hand on my shoulder while I read. Another student approached me and asked if she could share one of her favorite stories, told to her by her Diné grandmother, about how the Big Dipper came to be." She went on to tell me about the shifts that began to occur across her program as a direct result of this book.

Hello, Neighbor: The Kind and Caring World of Mister Rogers by Matthew Cordell

This is the story of Fred McFeely Rogers, a person who had a big impact on me as a child and still does as an adult. I associate watching *Mister Rogers' Neighborhood* with my kindergarten self. His name is probably common to many adults, but today's children may not be as familiar with him and his legacy. In the first authorized picture book biography of Fred Rogers, Caldecott Medalist Matthew Cordell details Fred's life from a lonely student who often felt as though he did not fit in, to an adult who created one of the most successful children's programs of all time.

APPLICATION TO STORY AS CLARIFIER

In addition to being a picture book biography that tells readers about Fred Rogers and his acclaimed television program, *Mister Rogers' Neighborhood*, this book shows how holding your beliefs as a compass, despite what others say, can help you reach your goals. You see Rogers' desire to use television as a positive medium that made children feel understood and validated while meeting them at their developmental level and, in this way, helping generations clarify their place in the worldwide community.

One Little Bag by Henry Cole

This wordless picture book chronicles the life of a single paper bag from tree, to pulp, to paper, to bag. A brown paper lunch bag, adorned with a single red heart, does more than contain the main character's lunch. It follows him through the stages of his life and changes as he changes, finally coming full circle. Henry Cole's author-illustrator's note tells of the single paper bag with which he carried his lunch to school the very first Earth Day. He proceeded to use it for years after; it served as the inspiration for this heartwarming story.

APPLICATION TO STORY AS CLARIFIER

One Little Bag heightens the reader's awareness of how quickly we dispose of items that are tossed aside while still usable. It allows the reader to consider the difference that would be made in our world if only we realized the potential of one little bag and weren't so quick to throw it (or other objects) away when there is still much life left to them. On a larger scale, the book's theme reminds us to consider the effects our actions and decisions can have on others in our community.

The Oldest Student: How Mary Walker Learned to Read by Rita Lorraine Hubbard; illustrated by Oge Mora

Mary Walker was enslaved until she was fifteen. She had a lifelong dream to learn to read. Throughout her life, there were things that caused her to postpone, but never abandon, her dream. At the age of 114, Mary decided it was time to make her dream come true. She enrolled in classes to learn to read. This beautifully illustrated book tells of her rich life and celebrates her accomplishments.

APPLICATION TO STORY AS CLARIFIER

Despite the difficulties she faced, *The Oldest Student* shows Mary Walker's joy and passion as she worked to reach her goals. The reader sees how she put the needs of her family before her own dreams and, despite great sadness in her life, did not give up. She continued forward with a joyful heart. Mary shows us that we're never too old to learn and to follow our passions and interests.

The Next President: The Unexpected Beginnings and Unwritten Future of America's Presidents by Kate Messner; illustrated by Adam Rex

This is not your ordinary nonfiction book detailing the often dull history of past presidents of the United States. Kate Messner emphasizes that although there is only one president at any given time, there are many future presidents walking among us. As she highlights the differences in past presidents—such as some liked adventure, one ran a peanut farm, and many owned unusual animals—she also points out the one thing that most had in common, that they were almost all white men. Messner emphasizes that things are changing and stresses that the door is open to anyone who meets the qualifications—regardless of gender or color—and could even be the reader.

This witty and informative book challenges common beliefs about the presidency. There is always one president in office, but many future presidents are leading exciting and interesting lives, acquiring the skills to one day become president. *The Next President* encourages readers to dream about what the future might hold. And it's an exciting thing to consider.

Dragon Hoops by Gene Luen Yang

Dragon Hoops, written and illustrated by former National Ambassador for Young People's Literature Gene Luen Yang, is a graphic novel that follows the Bishop O'Dowd High School basketball team as they seek a state championship. It is a story about Gene, who taught at Bishop O'Dowd; the history of basketball; the individual players on the team; and the past and present coaches. As much as it is a book about basketball, it is also about humanity, the stories each of us carries, and the impact each of our stories has on our actions.

APPLICATION TO STORY AS CLARIFIER

From an outward appearance, *Dragon Hoops* appears to be a book about basketball; however, it is so much more. It teaches the reader something unexpected—it looks past the action of the game to the individual players and their stories as well as the stories of those who helped make the game what it is today.

The Bridge Home by Padma Venkatraman

Dr. Padma Venkatraman tells the story of Viji and Rukku, sisters who run away from their home in Chennai, India, to avoid an abusive father. Viji and Rukku quickly learn it is difficult to survive on the streets alone and have to learn to trust others if they are to survive.

Also a great book for compassion and connection, this story sheds light on the difficulty of being a child living on the streets of India and the many challenges these children face. It exposes the reader to a myriad of social issues to which they may be unaware. Although a fictional story, it heightens the reader's awareness of the hardships faced by many and allows them to empathize with the characters as well as those facing these situations in real life. As Padma (2019) shared on the Nerdy Book Club's blog, "Novels that invite us to travel to other places can do much more than transport the reader to another location; they can transform the reader by allowing the reader to experience the culture from within. When we see not only through the narrator's lens, but also from within the narrator's soul, when we live for a little while in another part of the world by living inside a character's skin, we start, slowly, in small ways, to become citizens of the world."

Honeybee: The Busy Life of Apis Mellifera by Candace Fleming; illustrated by Eric Rohmann

This is the story of the complex life of a worker bee. Candace Fleming craftily lays out the many stages of this industrious bee's life, allowing the reader to understand the dedication and tenacity this small bee has and the incredible feats it completes during its short life. The author's note at the end illustrates the anatomy of the worker bee and how each part of its body assists it in completing a necessary task. It also teaches the reader how to help protect honeybees and where to go to learn more.

This is the perfect book for your student who always wants more information about a topic they feel passionately about. If that child is interested in bees, this is the book for them! It explores the many jobs worker bees have and details just how they complete each job. It shows how one tiny bee carries out tasks that seem insurmountable to the reader but are, in reality, just a regular part of the life of a honeybee. If after reading *Honeybee* the reader wants even more information, Candace recommends books and websites where they can continue learning about this remarkable insect.

Kent State by Deborah Wiles

This novel in verse details the Kent State shootings as well as the days leading up to them. It is told from multiple perspectives and allows the reader insight into each person's unique viewpoint. Although the events unfolded fifty years prior, Wiles expertly demonstrates how they are just as relevant today.

APPLICATION TO STORY AS CLARIFIER

This story invites the reader to see people differently and thus view this event differently. The shooting is one part of the story. As we come to understand the many facets that led up to the shooting and meet the townspeople, the students, the National Guard, Deborah Wiles subtly invites us to see how this event has implications with today's social situations.

We Are Water Protectors by Carole Lindstrom; illustrated by Michaela Goade

This stunningly illustrated and poetically told tale is based on an Anishinaabe prophecy. It shows the importance of water in all aspects of life and how all things are interconnected; what impacts one impacts all. It tells of the black snake that endangers Earth and all creatures that inhabit it. This prophecy parallels the oil line that threatens the land in North Dakota and shows the urgency that we speak up to protect this sacred water and all who depend on it. Carole Lindstrom is Anishinabe/Métis and is enrolled with the Turtle Mountain Band of Ojibwe, and Michaela Goade is an enrolled member of the Tlingit and Haida Indian Tribes of Alaska and is of the Kiks.ádi Clan from Sikta, Alaska.

APPLICATION TO STORY AS CLARIFIER

This story heightens the reader's awareness of the Standing Rock Water Protectors who are committed to saving the Earth, and all its creatures, from damage caused by the Dakota Access Pipeline. It invites them to join this fight and pledge to be stewards committed to protecting the water that nourishes us all. As Carole Lindstrom (2020) shared when I interviewed her on my blog, "We hope *We Are Water Protectors* inspires you to protect our sacred planet and give back to Mother Earth, to support and join Water Protectors/Land Defenders around the world. No action is too small. Together we are strong. Mni Wiconi! Water is life."

My favorite titles for story as clarifier

CHAPTER

Story as Compassion

At the 2020 Democratic National Convention, former First Lady Michelle Obama reminded us of the importance of moving from feelings to action, arguing that doing so "is the truest form of empathy; not just feeling, but doing; not just for yourselves, but for everyone, for all our kids." I've been carrying around these words inside my heart since then and keep circling back to them, thinking about how they perfectly sum up my feelings about story as compassion. The way I see it, compassion is more than empathy because it moves us beyond our feelings and into a desire to make change.

#StoryIs

"Story is a way to grow empathy, a way to discover how much we share, despite our differences."

SUPRIYA KELKAR, AUTHOR OF
THAT THING ABOUT BOLLYWOOD

When we're engrossed in story, it's often easy to get lost in our feelings and rest there. As a highly sensitive person, this is something I love about experiencing story. I feel deeply. Sometimes, however, I get so caught up with my feelings and emotions that I forget to take action—to actually do something that can bring about change. This idea of compassion evolves as we experience the other affective elements of story we've discussed so far. When we get to know ourselves and others better, as we learn to heal old wounds, and as we investigate our curiosities, we are often inspired by our emotions to take action.

Students come to us with caring hearts, and when we let the books we share set the right conditions, story can help them access this compassion. When we introduce our students to characters and historical figures who lead and work with compassion, they are more likely to work to make the world a better, more just place. This often goes beyond any surface level concept of "making the world a better place" to include specific actions. I think about the fourth graders I met in Michigan, who after reading Katherine Applegate's (2015) *Crenshaw*, held a food drive and volunteered at food pantries. I'm reminded of my former third graders who, after reading Jonathan London and Jon Van Zyle's (2004) *The Eyes of Gray Wolf*, wrote letters to their state senators and local congresspeople urging them to please support legislation that would help protect gray wolves.

This ties perfectly into Kelly Barnhill's idea of what she calls radical empathy. In an interview the week after she won the 2017 Newbery Medal for *The Girl Who Drank the Moon* (2016), I asked her to finish the sentence starter, "Story is . . ." She responded with, "Story is an act of radical empathy—by shedding my skin and bones and experience and taking on the skin and bones and experience of another, I am forced to confront the limitations of my own point of view" (2017). Often, when we allow ourselves to access this type of radical empathy, it drives us toward taking the next logical step to bring about change in our environments. Though stories can help us explore and better understand our own hearts and humanity, they can also help us harness our reactions and feelings to make a difference in our lives, the lives of others, and the world around us.

From the Brain to the Heart

In an interview with Abigail Fagan (2021), psychologist Dr. Keith Oatley states, "As you identify with another person, a protagonist in the story, you enter into a piece of life that you wouldn't have known. You have emotions or circumstances you wouldn't have otherwise understood." Although all of this may seem more grounded in heart work—and it is—it may also surprise you to know that scientists have been studying this connection for some time. For instance, Dr. Uri Hasson (Svoboda 2015), a professor in the Department of Psychology and the Neuroscience Institute at Princeton University, studied fMRI (functional magnetic resonance imaging) scans and discovered that when we listen to someone else tell their stories, our brains activate in the same way as the storyteller and map on to their experiences. In a discussion of this work and other fMRI studies, Elizabeth Svoboda (2015) summarizes the findings saying, "The fMRI data showed that

#StoryIs

"Story is essential for growing and learning and becoming more thoughtful and compassionate humans. It is in our nature to share stories and connect with each other through them—throughout our whole lives."

Jo Knowles, author of *Ear Worm*

emotion-driven responses to stories like these started in the brain stem, which governs basic physical functions, such as digestion and heartbeat. So when we read about a character facing a heart-wrenching situation, it's perfectly natural for our own hearts to pound."

We also know from mirror neuron research that when we observe the actions of others, we unconsciously feel and simulate empathetic responses (Flasbeck, Gonzalez-Liencres, and Brüne 2018). This resonates when we think about the power of visual imagery that story evokes in us and our students. The best stories and the most powerful read-alouds bring to life an image in our minds that we observe, and through that observation, we experience a biological jolt of empathy. Think about the implications this has on the books we share, the books we read aloud, and the stories we invite our students to experience.

In their contribution to the book *Compassion and Empathy in Educational Contexts*, Georgina Barton, Margaret Baguley, and Abby McDonald (2019) cite studies that highlight the effect images and language can have on our emotions through conversations about books and studying the craft found in children's books. They point out research-based supports for how sharing stories can lead to positive effects on:

- self-awareness and management
- social-awareness and management
- the effects our actions have on others
- interpersonal relationships
  (as opposed to individualistic thinking)

This is a valuable reminder of the power of the books we share with students and how they offer, as the authors say, "an important opportunity to provide them with the skills and abilities to respond in ways that are critical for their future" (185).

Emotionally, sharing our hearts through story can resonate a message of the important qualities that bring our hearts together in a humanistic way. In *Why You Should Read Children's Books, Even Though You Are So Old and Wise*, Dr. Katherine Rundell (2019) reminds us, "Children's books say: the world is huge. They say: hope counts for something. They say: bravery will matter, wit will matter, empathy will matter, love will matter" (48).

Voices From

Guidance counselor turned school librarian, Deirdre Iuliani, embodies this connection between story and humanity in both her career choices and the way she thinks about the books she includes in her collection and the stories she shares with students at Merriam Avenue Elementary School in New Jersey.

Deirdre Iuliani

Literature has the ability to unite our diverse human experiences. A well-written story has a peculiar way of encouraging self-discovery while simultaneously connecting us to others. The subtle process by which this happens can have far-reaching personal and global benefits, yet oftentimes will go unnoticed.

Stories target our affective state by influencing our ability to empathize with others. When we have empathy for others, we can feel or understand how someone else might be feeling. This is often done by gathering clues from facial features and body language, listening to what others are saying and how they are saying it, as well as considering the context or circumstances of the situation. Asking ourselves how we might feel in a similar situation helps us experience a shift away from ourselves toward a deeper connection with others.

Let's consider Jacqueline Woodson's (2012) Each Kindness, illustrated by E. B. Lewis, as an example. Maya enters her new classroom with her shoulders slumped, her head bowed toward the floor, her eyes looking down, and in a barely

audible voice whispers hello. The author goes on to describe Maya's clothes as old and ragged and her shoes broken and inappropriate for the current season. At this very early point in the book, readers are able to use clues to understand that Maya comes from circumstances quite different than the rest of the students. Regardless, they continue to isolate rather than welcome her. It isn't until much later in the story that the protagonist starts to think about how Maya might be feeling.

While having empathy is certainly the cornerstone of being a decent human being, acts of compassion can serve as a bridge between understanding how someone feels and making a genuine effort to connect with them. Compassion is when we show care or concern for another by doing something kind or helpful.  A Sick Day for Amos McGee written by Philip C. Stead (2010), illustrated by Erin E. Stead, shows the impact a compassionate act can have on a developing relationship. Amos McGee is a kindhearted soul who visits with his animal friends regularly. The animals grow quite worried when Amos doesn't show up one day and decide to visit him only to learn he is feeling under the weather. The animals put together a plan to take care of Amos while keeping him company at the same time. At this point in the story, the animals are putting empathy into action.

Empathy helps us understand and appreciate our human differences. The ability to show compassion is evidence that we can be tolerant and accepting of these differences. Story has the power to challenge and alter our own perspectives similar to the way an author challenges the feelings and viewpoints of a character. For example, in El Deafo, Cece Bell's (2014) character is a typical kid who happens to wear a hearing aid. This graphic novel brings to light issues Cece Bell has experienced firsthand as a person living with a hearing impairment that other children might not experience in the same way. Readers who identify with a character like Cece might find their own feelings validated. They might find it "safer" to talk about the character's situation than their own, thus making the discussion less threatening, yet still personally meaningful. They might find this story is exactly what they need to practice self-compassion while their peers gain a better understanding of compassion toward others.

The undeniable power of story as compassion is that it connects us globally. It assists us with opening our hearts to understanding the value other cultures bring to our world. In Fry Bread: A Native American Family Story by Kevin Noble Maillard (2019), illustrated by Juana Martinez-Neal, Maillard uses fry bread to represent the beliefs and traditions of a modern Native American family. To extend the message of the story even further, Maillard provides a recipe for readers to make their own fry bread at the end of the book. When an author allows a reader to be immersed in another culture's tradition, the author creates a powerful opportunity for the reader to participate in something much bigger than the reader's experience.

We live in a world where we are bombarded with constant reminders that our society tends to lack empathy and the ability to show compassion. Fortunately for us, empathy and compassion can be taught. And while this discussion was limited to picture books, readers should be encouraged to know that authors of every type of literature are helping to continue this important work. Using story as a connection to compassion is one of the best tools we currently have at our disposal.

#StoryIs

"Story is what unites us, all. When we enter a story and climb into the skins of its characters, we discover how alike we humans really are. No matter what we look like on the outside, we all laugh and cry, experience joy and despair, and are all enriched by the love we have in our lives. As we learn through story how alike we are, the walls we've built between us begin to crumble, and those walls are replaced by a little thing called compassion."

NIKKI GRIMES, AUTHOR OF *KAMALA HARRIS: ROOTED IN JUSTICE*

From the Heart to the Classroom

When we turn our attention to direct classroom applications, we find multiple avenues for applying Deirdre's comments. For instance, language arts teachers probably noticed direct connections between her comments about recognizing facial expressions and standard inference studies that support comprehension like paying attention to dialogue, character motivations, and how those affect comprehension. This again hints to the inextricable connections between the academic and affective elements of story introduced in Chapter 1.

Reading Without Walls

During Gene Luen Yang's two-year term as the National Ambassador for Young People's Literature, he traveled around the United States sharing the importance of Reading Without Walls (Yang 2016b), reminding us, "Reading is a fantastic way to open your minds and hearts to new people, places, and ideas. Through reading, I've met new friends, learned new facts, and become a better person" (Library of Congress 2016). Gene's mission and platform live on beyond his term as ambassador. Encourage your students and colleagues to participate in the Reading Without Walls Challenge by:

1. Reading a book about a character who doesn't look like them or live like them

2. Reading a book about a topic they don't know much about

3. Reading a book in a format they don't normally read for fun (a chapter book, a graphic novel, a book in verse, or an audio book)

Think about the opportunities this simple invitation affords us—as individual readers and as learning communities. For many of our students, it doesn't dawn on them to reach beyond their own experiences and explore others' experiences. Without that exploration, we cannot begin to empathize in a compassionate way. It falls to us to give that gentle nudge as we build and promote inclusive book collections, because as Gene Luen Yang shared when I interviewed him, "The stories humans tell are a long conversation about what it means to be human. This conversation extends across cultures and generations. It began when we began and won't end until we end. By writing stories, I participate in that conversation" (2016a).

"Now What?" Questions

Some of the best and most meaningful memories I have from my time as a classroom teacher and as a teacher-librarian center around when a word, a passage, or an illustration from a story resulted in a lengthy and eye-opening and meaningful dialogue that prompted further reflections about how the text made us feel. So often, this

You can find out more about Gene Luen Yang and his wonderful mission by scanning this code:

#StoryIs

"Story is sacred. Story is everywhere. Stories make us human, build empathy, and bring us together. If I know someone's story, I find myself connected with them in a way that transcends my own selfishness and breaks down barriers. Stories saved my life growing up."

CHRIS BARON, AUTHOR OF *THE MAGICAL IMPERFECT*

began simply enough with specific observations that nudged us to consider "now what?" Young readers often don't give themselves permission to take action based on a reading experience. To support this, we can model and invite students to act when they feel—not in every instance, but when the heart calls. Share with students those moments when you put a book down and said to yourself, "I must act on this. I must do something. I must share and discuss this." This makes me think of Lisa Fipps's (2021) *Starfish*. Readers come to know the main character, Ellie, through her actions and reactions to the words others use. Her story, based on Lisa's own childhood experiences of being bullied about her weight, gives us an opportunity to go even deeper to think about our personal feelings about body image and bullying.

Starfish was originally written as a young adult novel in verse. Nancy Paulsen, Lisa's brilliant editor, suggested she, instead, rewrite it as a middle-grade novel in verse to reach kids who were currently being bullied about their weight. She thought the story could give younger readers the courage and tools to stand up for themselves. And as Lisa writes in her acknowledgments, "And maybe, just maybe, *Starfish* would reach the bullies and get them to stop."

There's a poem in the book I know learning communities could lose hours discussing. It shows the power of story, and it lends itself to conversations about story as compassion. Here is an excerpt from the poem:

> In English class,
> Mrs. Boardman asks
> us to sum up what we've read with
> our favorite quotes from the book.
>
> I know just the quote
> from *Song for a Whale*.
> I raise my hand and
> she calls on me.
> "The whale 'didn't need to be fixed.
> He was the whale who
> sang his own song'
> That really hit home.
> That's what the best books do.
> They make you think,
> and rethink
> how you see
> yourself,
> others,
> and the world.
> Most of all,
> they make you feel.
> Feelings toward people
> who aren't like you.
> Feelings you didn't know
> you had."

And that's what story does for us: it pushes us to think empathetically about others and even ourselves, moves us from reaction to action, and shows us how to make the world a better place. It drives us into those "now what?" moments that leave us changed and ready to see things differently.

Mr. Schu Suggests

Whether it's *Starfish, Song for a Whale* (Kelly 2019), books from your own collection, or one from a list of my favorites that follows, consider ways story can move you and your readers beyond empathy and into compassion.

This Way, Charlie by Caron Levis; illustrated by Charles Santoso

This is the story of two animals at the Open Bud Ranch, an animal rehabilitation center, that form an unlikely and touching friendship. Jack is a goat who likes to keep to himself until a vision-impaired horse named Charlie arrives. They form a friendship that becomes even stronger as Charlie's vision worsens and Jack helps his friend by becoming his eyes, and in turn Charlie helps heal his wounds.

APPLICATION TO STORY AS COMPASSION

This story shows how friends help each other, even when helping is uncomfortable and scary. The reader understands that friends take each other as they are without judgment and are willing to weather difficult times as well as joyful times. It illustrates how compassion and gentleness can help heal even the deepest of wounds.

Dreamers by Yuyi Morales

This story chronicles Yuyi Morales's move from Mexico to the United States. It follows her as she navigates the difficult transition to her new life in the United States. What began as a difficult and lonely journey turned around due to the compassion and kindness she encountered at the public library— interactions that helped her become who she is today.

APPLICATION TO STORY AS COMPASSION

Through this story, students learn that even small compassion-ate gestures can make a significant difference. They learn how a kind word and a simple gesture, such as welcoming someone to the library and giving them a library card, can have effects that last for years.

Encourage students to find the two snakes Yuyi hid in the book. Why did she include snakes? Yuyi (2018) answers, "They represent thoughts, feelings and experiences that might be difficult or scary for us, but if we look hard, we would see that those same fears make us grow, and be better and more compassionate walkers on this earth."

The Day You Begin by Jacqueline Woodson; illustrated by Rafael López

This is the story of new beginnings and how they can be scary. New faces with whom you think you share nothing in common, new people whose lives appear vastly different from yours, new friends who may find the food you eat strange, and the feelings that can make you feel even more like an outsider. *The Day You Begin* eloquently highlights how, to feel like an insider, you must find the courage to tell your story and to share yourself. Only then will you begin to feel connected to those new faces that surround you.

APPLICATION TO STORY AS COMPASSION

This book shows the feelings a new student at school experiences. It helps children build compassion as they begin to think how their new classmates might feel and how their unintentional actions can both hurt and help that student feel included or excluded. It reminds the reader that we all have a story, things that we share in common and things that we have that are different, but it is only when we begin sharing our stories that these can be discovered and we can begin to build community.

The Power of One: Every Act of Kindness Counts by Trudy Ludwig; illustrated by Mike Curato

This story begins with a simple picture of a person yelling at another person and making them upset. It then follows the transformation that occurs when one person reaches out and causes a ripple effect. It demonstrates the power that a single person and a single simple gesture have to cause lasting change.

APPLICATION TO STORY AS COMPASSION

This book highlights how the simplest act of compassion can cause lasting change. The author's note provides concrete ways readers can reach out and work for change by themselves. This book empowers people to see their value in making the world better and how it can begin with something as simple as one kind act.

The People's Painter: How Ben Shahn Fought for Justice with Art by Cynthia Levinson; illustrated by Evan Turk

This is the story of artist Ben Shahn who, even as a young boy in Lithuania, had a strong sense of wrong and right and refused to stay quiet in the face of injustice. It follows Ben as he immigrates with his family to the United States, struggles to find happiness in this new land, and is forced to drop out of school to help his family survive. His passion for social justice and art never subsides; Ben is able to find a way to combine the two, becoming a successful and important artist, despite the criticism he faced.

APPLICATION TO STORY AS COMPASSION

Ben Shahn felt the need from a very early age to speak out for what is right. Readers see how he used his passion for art to tell the story of people in difficult circumstances and help make their struggles known. Readers learn they can use their interests—be it art, music, writing—to show compassion by telling the stories of those individuals who are marginalized or facing other unfortunate circumstances.

Wishes by Mượn Thị Văn; illustrated by Victo Ngai

Wishes is a gentle picture book that subtly, yet powerfully, illustrates the hardships faced by a family about to flee Vietnam. It is based on Mượn's family's experience as refugees. She shared the following with me in an interview: "I hope *Wishes* opens hearts and minds. I wanted the reader to be able to see, and feel, the story from the inside and I hope we succeeded" (2020).

APPLICATION TO STORY AS COMPASSION

Readers can't help but feel moved as they progress through this book, realizing that the family in it is about to embark on a treacherous journey, nor can readers help but wonder why they are leaving and putting themselves in such danger. As they read the author's note, the pieces fall in place, allowing the reader to feel compassion for the bravery and struggle this family, and the author's family, experienced. It's also an opportunity to look at our own wishes and realize that, although important to us, they are often minute compared with the wishes of those faced with situations such as these.

Lala's Words by Gracey Zhang

Lala is unlike others in her neighborhood. To the dismay of her mother, she refuses to stay home in the heat and instead spends her days in an unkept lot talking to the weeds she treats as treasured friends. She gives them encouragement to grow and prosper, showering love and kindness upon them as though they were human friends. Finally forced to stay home by her mother, away from her beloved plants, Lala and her mom are amazed at an unexpected happening that illustrates the power of love.

APPLICATION TO STORY AS COMPASSION

Compassion is shown as Lala speaks encouraging words to the plants in the lot. Although this act may appear insignificant, it isn't. Readers are subtly reminded of the power of words and the miraculous things that can happen when we use our words to build each other up and encourage each other. We're also reminded how compassion is reciprocated.

☻ *Your Name Is a Song* by Jamilah Thompkins-Bigelow; illustrated by Luisa Uribe

The story opens with a child upset because many of her classmates and her teacher cannot pronounce her name on the first day of school. Her mother empowers her to speak out and sing her beautiful name as a way of teaching it to others. In teaching her daughter to advocate for herself, she also teaches her the power and beauty in names.

APPLICATION TO STORY AS COMPASSION

This book beautifully illustrates the idea that compassion is also something one does for themselves. Students see the main character gracefully advocate for herself as she gathers the courage to teach others how to say her name. They learn that, even though scary, advocating for themselves is an important thing to do. Readers will be inspired to speak up for themselves instead of remaining quiet as they may have in the past.

☻ *Gone to the Woods: Surviving a Lost Childhood* by Gary Paulsen

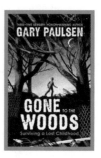

This memoir recounts five distinctive periods in three-time Newbery Honor–winning author Gary Paulsen's life. It details a difficult childhood and adolescence and his uncanny ability to look within himself and in nature to find the determination to not only survive but also to succeed.

APPLICATION TO STORY AS COMPASSION

The reader will be stunned at the many difficulties Gary Paulsen faced while growing up and will see compassion in many of the adults he encounters along the way. Gary specifically recalls the compassion shown to him by a librarian who he credits with changing his life. Readers see how compassion can be quiet and gentle and seemingly insignificant at the time, yet can have lasting and even life-changing results, and how simple acts of kindness and understanding are remembered many years later. They, in turn, learn the impact even simple acts of kindness can have and are motivated to show kindness to others.

 *Land of the Cranes* by Aida Salazar

Nine-year-old Betita listened closely to her Papi's tales about Aztlán, the land of their ancestors and the land of the cranes. This theme is woven throughout the story Betita tells of her loving family, her Papi's deportation, and ultimately the experiences she and her Mami experience in a detention center. Salazar (2020) hopes *Land of the Cranes* "reaches readers' hearts and minds and serves to expand their capacity for empathy and love, but also to understand the need for compassionate justice for migrants."

APPLICATION TO STORY AS COMPASSION

Through this free-verse novel, readers learn of the cruel and inhumane treatment given to many undocumented residents. They see the cruelty of denying basic needs such as water and heat. They also experience compassion as Mami tells Betita that it is always important to do "what our hearts tell us is right." This simple statement teaches the reader to follow their hearts, speak up, and take action when they see something they know is wrong.

My favorite titles for story as compassion

6
CHAPTER

Story as Connector

I t feels as though every moment spent writing this book of my heart has been leading me, guiding me toward this chapter. No doubt you've started to notice that though we've unpacked the affective elements of story individually, they're all intricately connected. So, it's fitting that we wrap things up with a final chapter about story as connector. Each element is like a spoke on a wheel—each connected to one another, to us, to our stories, and to humanity. This brings to mind an anonymous letter I received in 2019.

Dear Mr. Schu,

I'm an intervention specialist who had the pleasure of attending one of your presentations last year. You gifted a book to one of my second graders. You could have not chosen a more grateful recipient.

As a baby, this student had a severe illness which left her with a significant cognitive impairment. Her parents have fostered a love of books in her, and she's worked very hard to become a proficient reader. Being able to read chapter books is not only a source of pride for her, but also one of the joys of her life. Upon receiving the book you gave her, she hugged it to her heart and didn't let it go. Her mother related that she continued to hug it all the way home and couldn't wait to read it to her family upon arrival. If you ever need confirmation of the importance of how your work connects with students, please remember the gift you gave this child. It is a gift neither she nor I will ever forget!

Thank you,
A Grateful Teacher

I don't know which school this letter came from or the name of the child, but I know this: her heart needed *that* book, and it found its way to her because we connected through story. There is this hard-to-describe sensation, one that feels magical and palpable, that presents itself when a group gathers to celebrate and read stories together. I have experienced it in classrooms, in libraries, and with 200 fourth graders in an auditorium. It's heart-growing and it can be life-changing.

It's as if we send out *light* when we talk about something we care deeply and passionately about—when we speak from the heart. For me, it's when I discuss and share the power and importance of story. It's when I lift up and celebrate books full of light and laughter, love and hope. It's when I share my own stories and the stories of others. But then something miraculous happens: as others respond, as they open up their hearts, they give off beams and bursts of that same type of light. That light, that energy, enters the room and hearts start to open and to connect. You can feel it. You can see it.

For a long time, I kept these experiences to myself. They felt way too woo-woo to share. It wasn't until I read a feature story a few years ago in *The New York Times* (Sehgal 2019) that I felt comfortable enough sharing my own experiences. In an interview, Tony Award–winning actor Glenda Jackson relates that, to her way of thinking, the two most powerful words are *only connect*, and she goes on to discuss an energy that's produced from oneself and sent out into the dark during a performance. The audience receives the light and then sends it back. She refers to it as "the model of an ideal society incumbent on everyone working together. It doesn't always happen, but it has happened enough to know that it's possible." This is connection. This is story as connector. This is how we ultimately grow through the stories we read and the stories we share.

#StoryIs

"Stories are energy and balm. They heal and save. They are electric and energetic. They lift you up— make you feel like you are part of a community. Stories connect us to each other—they are a bridge for our experiences."

ELLEN HAGAN, AUTHOR OF *RECKLESS, GLORIOUS, GIRL*

From the Brain to the Heart

Kate DiCamillo isn't a neuroscientist or a research psychologist, but from reading all of her books, speeches, and Facebook updates, you wonder if she has a PhD in Connection. She has her thumb on the pulse of the human heart. She ponders and observes how the heart connects through story in profound ways. In an interview with The Children's Book Council (2014), she shared, "We are all connected by stories because we are stories ourselves. There's that wonderful quote from Muriel Rukeyser: *the universe isn't made of atoms. It is made of stories.* When we learn someone else's story, it shifts the fabric of our being. We are more open. And when we are open, we connect."

George Saunders, a professor of writing at Syracuse University and a National Book Award finalist, sees similar patterns of interpersonal connections through the lens of a story like a laboratory that helps us see our own habits and projections. When we read a story, we're able to connect with the person who wrote it. While writing *A Swim in the Pond in the Rain* (Saunders 2021), he realized that "when you're reading a story and analyzing it, you're really reassuring

PHOTOGRAPH BY ERIELLE BAKKUM

#StoryIs

"Story is connection. I believe stories are one of the most amazing forms of interrelatedness that we've ever created. Since humans first began using images, since our earliest days of language, we've used stories to share who we are, to explain our world, to understand ourselves, to know one another. Story telling is a core part of human existence. And when I consider all the stories we've created, across time, across cultures and languages, I'm in awe of how wondrous we are."

SAMIRA AHMED, *NEW YORK TIMES* BESTSELLING AUTHOR OF *LOVE, HATE & OTHER FILTERS, INTERNMENT,* AND *AMIRA & HAMZA: THE WAR TO SAVE THE WORLDS*

yourself that connection is possible" (Fox 2021). We often feel the most open to the world after we read the last page of an amazing story. In *A Swim in the Pond in the Rain*, Saunders states, "There are many versions of you, in you. To which one am I speaking when I write? The best one. The one most like my best one. Those two best versions of us, in a moment of reading, exit our usual selves and, at a location created by mutual respect, become one" (389).

Lisa Cron, who has written a whole book about the way brain science connects to the power of story, said in an interview with *The Agency Review*, "One of the things I love about neuroscience is that so often it proves what writers always knew. Writers were the first neuroscientists, except then it was seen as metaphor. For instance, take the notion that the pen is mightier than the sword. Science has revealed that the power of words to shape the reality we see goes far beyond anything we've ever imagined" (2014). This circles back to DiCamillo's and Saunders's earlier thoughts on connection and encourages us to consider how stories bring neuroscience and hearts into the same space with dramatic effects.

Voices From

THE PRINCIPAL'S DESK

Up to this point, we've focused on the role teachers and teacher-librarians play in nurturing the reading lives of their students. It's no secret that campus administrators play a vital role as well—especially in driving initiatives toward creating environments that invite reading connections across classrooms, grade levels, entire buildings—and, ultimately, hearts. Kelly Gustafson, the principal at Wexford Elementary School, and Dr. Laquita Outlaw, the former principal at Bayshore Middle School and current assistant superintendent of the Bay Shore School District, are advocates for literacy on their campuses and for the reading lives of faculty, staff, and the children they work with every day.

I believe, to create a connected community of readers, we should model an excitement for reading. Elementary students need to be surrounded by a culture of adults discovering and discussing story. Knowing the impact we have on our youngest readers when adults share books with colleagues or students, we work hard in the Wexford Elementary School office to connect stories with readers.

Elementary school life is busy. Everyone is moving at a fast pace and has a purpose in their walk. My challenge as an instructional leader was to slow people down so they could reflect past clouds of to-do lists in their heads and take time to consider books they might share with their learning communities. I tried starting or ending grade-level and faculty meetings with booktalks, but I worried that it came across less as an encouraging "you should check this out" interaction and more as a formal directive. This makes sense. Faculty meetings are often packed with new items to discuss and longer lists of urgent tasks to check off during the week. Very few adults walked out of the meeting with one of my books in their stack of papers.

Watching the faculty arrive in the school office each morning to check in and discuss the day's activities, I noticed they were relaxed and enjoyed each other's conversation as they checked in about their teaching plans and suggestions for learning activities. This atmosphere of casual interaction gave me an idea.

I started by decorating the table adjacent to the faculty mailboxes with three picture books, a chapter book, and a professional development text such as Donalyn Miller's The Book Whisperer (2009). I turned the colorful cover art so that it conveniently faced the faculty members, greeting them as they signed in for the day. This Principal's Lending Library grew to be a place where adults gathered, browsed book options, and carried titles to their classrooms. Books didn't need to be signed out and could anonymously be returned if it wasn't a fit, and the strategic location increased the amount of books my faculty was able to explore.

Eventually, I refined the Principal's Lending Library by pairing the selections with email recommendations about a featured author or illustrator. This concept evolved into a Grab & Go area of our elementary office. Teachers stashed away books to take home to family members or grabbed them on their way to class to review for a possible read-aloud selection. I could tell I had a hit on my hands when the decorated table was empty by dismissal time.

I challenged myself to extend the success of the Grab & Go concept even further by featuring the selections at the monthly PTO meetings. At each meeting during the conclusion of my Principal's Report, I featured four book titles recommended for family bedtime or leisure reading together. Parents were encouraged to borrow the books as often as they'd like and have their child return it to me with a thumbs-up or thumbs-down review. It was important to pass the books around to the tables knowing if I could get the books into the hands of the most influential adults in a child's life, a parent, they'd be shared at home too. I knew it was working when I left the PTO meeting without having to carry any of the books back to the office! Soon, I began getting email messages from parents with photos of their child reading. It became a common occurrence for parent volunteers to stop me in the hallway or parking lot to discuss a recently featured book.

Soon, teachers and families were asking the school librarian to put holds on titles that were spotlighted in the office, and I was thrilled by this ripple effect. We are fortunate to have a library with multiple copies, curated by an enthusiastic school librarian. Since she was the single point of contact with our students, her expertise helped spread my passion for sharing stories to build relationships with them. This intentional two-point approach made a huge difference in our efforts. She focused on the students, and my target area was the adults; our connection met in the middle!

Recently, a teacher sent a text message with a picture of her colleague walking to bus duty while reading Katherine Applegate's (2012) The One and Only Ivan. She needed to finish it before she took the book home and shared it with her family members. And when Disney announced the book was being released as a movie, my inbox was flooded by parent celebrations.

Now, when students are waiting beside the book selections in the office, it's common to overhear the secretaries recommending a book with a teaser, "The principal thinks that one is too gross to read" or

"My kids and I couldn't put this one down!" Books can be found on the nurse's desk as well, so students who aren't feeling well can find distractions by poring over stories from Dav Pilkey's Dog Man series or talking over favorites with other students as they wait. Excitement flows through the hallways as third-grade and first-grade reading buddies talk about the illustrations, characters, or endings they discover in the pages together. And many students request familiar book titles recommended from the Principal's Lending Library for their birthday gifts.

From the school library, the teacher mailbox area, to PTO meetings, the secretaries' desks, and even the nurse's office, I'm always proud to share how the Wexford Elementary Community is meeting in the middle to share stories and make connections. And it all started with one big goal and a little idea.

LaQuita Outlaw

I am embarrassed to admit this, but my focus was
not always on literacy. Yes, as a secondary English
language arts teacher, I understand the importance
of learning to read. I also know how critical it is for
students—all students—to understand how to read to
learn. Though I knew the value of literacy in the lives
of the students that I served, it wasn't the message I
espoused when leading. It wasn't a part of my mantra. But, one chance
encounter changed all that—forever!

In 2015, School Library Journal, in partnership with Scholastic,
selected our librarian as the School Librarian of the Year. Of course,
I was thrilled for her because all of her hard work would now be
nationally recognized. The day for her recognition arrived, and she
invited me to meet the Scholastic representatives. It was a connection,
through books, that she knew I would find worthwhile. I planned to say
hello and return to the office to plug away at the piles of observations
and paperwork waiting on my desk to be done. I walked to the library
for that quick hello . . . but never returned to my piles.

I'm still not exactly sure what happened, but that day, something
clicked. Was it the former vice president of Scholastic Book Fairs
telling me that he didn't find a love for reading until high school?
Was it the reminder that it's never too late to light that spark in our
children? Did I, at that moment, realize the difference that I could
make in the specific reading lives of the many children that roam our
halls each day? I can't say. But what I can pinpoint is the difference
that one chance encounter made for the children in my building. That
connection changed the trajectory of my leadership and the way I
viewed the impact that story has on someone's life. The true passion
these visitors had for promoting independent reading was infectious—
and it was about more than just a book fair. I began to investigate
what other schools were doing to promote literacy, and the benefits

those practices yielded for the students they served, and I wanted that for my students as well.

It started with the "What are you reading?" signs. I loved the thought of teachers posting what they were reading for students to see—and this was an easy place to begin! I felt confident that it would either go really well, or it would go . . . well, it was optional. It could not go too poorly, right? I put my sign up first—and then several teachers followed. That one poster brought out the passion for reading in some staff that I never imagined. As it turned out, small signs promoting reading sparked something in both the adults and the students in the building. I was having conversations with teachers and students that I never had before. We were connecting in a deeper way, a different way. We were not talking about work; we were talking about stories, and we made connections through the books we were enjoying. More teachers joined in, and pretty soon, we had crowds of people talking about the books they were reading and asking for recommendations. To this very day, we still utilize the signs, except now we also include a picture of the book we just finished reading. This has added an additional layer to the connection, because we get to talk about two books instead of one.

The next simple step for me was to stand at my morning duty with a book in hand. I welcomed students with "Good morning" and stopped any child I saw with a book. We talked briefly, and once others began to see this, they too wanted to share the books they were reading. These casual morning booktalks eventually morphed into walking around the cafeteria with my book and talking with children about it. I started with the book Wonder by R. J. Palacio (2012). It was an instant hit. The students who had already read it were telling me how much I would love it, and there were a host of other children who were telling me that they wanted to read the book. This was another simple activity, but the benefits of promoting literacy in this way were huge. I must admit, the book selection was a significant part of the success of these activities.

I am forever grateful for the relationships and connections with students I have forged because of books.

After two successful activities promoting reading, I was hooked, and so were the students and staff. What would we do next? It did not take long to find an answer to that question. During a meeting with fellow principals, where we discussed how to help school leaders see the value of promoting reading, a Book Talk Challenge was issued. Again, this was a simple addition with significant results. I encouraged my staff to conduct book talks in their classes. I began to share my favorite reads over the PA system and then had the students and staff join in. We completed over 500 booktalks before the end of the school year!

We ended the school year with a door decorating contest. The staff was encouraged to pick a favorite book with their advisory (the class we also know as homeroom) and work together to recreate their favorite book's cover on their door. My door, created with the help of one of my esteemed art teachers, was inspired by Lynda Mullaly Hunt's (2015) Fish in a Tree, and it was the first to go up. Again, this activity was voluntary, but we had over sixty of ninety-nine advisories participate. The buzz around the building was palpable. We made sure to take pictures, and then students voted on their favorite door during lunch.

We still have a ways to go to ensure that literacy is a lasting, cultural practice in the school, but these few simple steps have us heading on the right path. I continue to be in awe of the stories teachers now share with me about the impact these activities have had on their classroom practice and on their relationships with kids. I hear about the connections teachers have made after reading a book a student recommended or the bonds they've developed with another child who never really interacted with them before. I cannot wait to see the opportunities to celebrate our reading lives and the reading lives of our students we come up with next.

From the Heart to the Classroom

Principals Kelly Gustafason and Dr. LaQuita Outlaw both implemented inspiring and concrete techniques to craft more positive stories about reading and the learning communities on their campuses. School-wide reading celebrations encourage everyone to celebrate books, cheer for books, and connect their stories to books. Here, I've compiled four of my favorite reading celebrations that help build positive reading communities for children.

International Dot Day

In Peter H. Reynolds's (2003) *The Dot*, Vashti's teacher tells her to "make a mark and see where it takes you." This invitation inspires Vashti, and *The Dot* inspires people all over the world on or around September 15th to collaborate, create, connect, and celebrate in honor of International Dot Day. My students and I made our mark and saw where it took us over the course of a week. We read and discussed *The Dot*. We used watercolors, finger paints, pencils, colored pencils, crayons, chalk, and iPads to make our mark inside and outside on the playground. We searched for dots in nature, wrote dot-inspired poetry, and ate DOTS. We wrapped up the week reading companion titles, *Ish* (Reynolds 2004) and *Sky Color* (Reynolds 2012). Together with *The Dot*, Peter calls them the "Creatiology," a trilogy focusing

For more ideas on how to celebrate International Dot Day, visit thedotclub.org.

on bravery, confidence, and creativity. In "A Classroom Guide to Peter H. Reynolds's Creatiology," he states, "All three stories provide encouragement for children—and grown-up children—to discover, explore, and develop their voice and express it in a unique way. It takes courage to do that, unfettered by self-doubt, unproductive feedback, or preconceived ideas" (Candlewick Press 2012).

World Read Aloud Day

There are times when you walk into a space and within a few moments you know it's an atmosphere that supports and promotes rich reading experiences and connecting through story. These types of libraries and classrooms buzz with conversation starters such as:

- ♥ What are you currently reading?

- ♥ What is it about this book that makes you love it?

- ♥ What was the last really good book you read?

- ♥ Who has read a fabulous book about dogs? How about a scary book? A funny book?

- ♥ Have you met these characters yet?

- ♥ What surprised you the most in this book?

- ♥ Wow, my heart was pounding hard toward the end of this book!

- ♥ Look at how the illustrations perfectly match the text!

- ♥ Do you have a moment? I want to tell you about these books.

- ♥ May I read aloud a passage from this book? I really want to know what you think of it.

The question that resonates the most with me is the last one. Think about the message it sends when we invite students into our reading lives and read aloud a book we love with them. Read to students. Discuss books. Experience stories together. When you do, you'll hear what they honestly think about books. Conversations like this stay firmly

Me at age seven, reading a favorite book

lodged in our memories. I believe I'm a reader today because my dear grandmother, first-grade teacher, second-grade teacher, and fifth-grade teacher shared their favorite stories with me. They conveyed the power of the read-aloud and how it connects us individually and with a group.

Take a few minutes to jot down the first read-aloud memories that come to your mind and think about how those experiences fed your reader's heart. I have so many connected moments that made me the reader I am today.

- ♥ It's 1986. I'm hugging a copy of *Goofy's Big Race* (Walt Disney 1985). I ask my grandma to read it to me just *one more time*. Please?! She, of course, reads it . . . two more times.

- ♥ It's 1987. I'm sitting on a bright blue carpet drinking chocolate milk. Miss Pollard plays the piano and then reads aloud from *Where the Sidewalk Ends* (Silverstein 1974). The music calms me and the poetry makes me laugh out loud.

- ♥ It's 1988. Mrs. Villender introduces us to Fern, Wilbur, Templeton, and Charlotte. I copy passages from *Charlotte's Web* (White 1952) into my diary. I fall in love with story. I want to write books one day.

- It's 1990. Dr. Reed reads aloud from Maurice Sendak's (1962) *Chicken Soup with Rice: A Book of Months*. I memorize every poem.

- It's 2004. I'm a fourth-grade teacher reading aloud *Out of the Dust* (Hesse 1997). I see eighteen teary-eyed students feeling Billie Jo's pain. You can hear a pin drop.

- It's 2011. A third-grade class is in the library virtually celebrating World Read Aloud Day with Laurel Snyder. She reads aloud a passage from *Penny Dreadful* (Snyder 2010). World Read Aloud Day becomes my favorite school-wide reading celebration.

Favorable read-aloud memories stir our desire to repeat similar experiences. Your students, too, have treasured read-aloud moments. Encourage them to share their favorites and create new ones together. A great way to get started with this habit is to share experiences together on World Read Aloud Day. And for the rest of their lives, your students will recall the excitement of hearing a children's book creator virtually read aloud their own writing or a classmate reading aloud one of their favorite books.

World Read Aloud Day takes place on the first Wednesday of every February. LitWorld and literacy expert Pam Allyn launched it in 2010 as a "celebration of the power of reading aloud to create community, to amplify new stories, and to advocate for literacy as a foundational human right. It has evolved into a global movement of millions of readers, writers, and listeners . . . coming together to honor the joy and power of reading and sharing stories" (LitWorld 2021).

PHOTOGRAPH BY SAM BOND

#StoryIs

"Story is what connects us to the people who came before and to the people we will become."

CHRISTINA SOONTORNVAT, AUTHOR OF
A WISH IN THE DARK

To get started on celebrating World Read Aloud Day, explore the following websites.

1. LitWorld (litworld.org/worldreadaloudday) created an activity hub dedicated to all things World Read Aloud Day. Download bookmarks, read-aloud games, and booklists, and view an archive of children's book creators reading aloud and sharing their work.

2. Award-winning author Kate Messner has a gift for connecting schools with authors and illustrators for virtual reading celebrations on World Read Aloud Day. Visit katemessner.com for more information.

3. Scholastic is a sponsor of World Read Aloud Day. Visit scholastic.com/worldreadaloudday to download a read-aloud advocate kit (WRADvocate), booklists, and the Scholastic Kids & Family Reading Report that includes a section about "The Rise of Read-Aloud." It reports that more than 80 percent of kids and caregivers "love or like read-aloud time because they consider it a special time together" (Allyn 2019). Scholastic also hosts the World Read Aloud Day Challenge. Connect with others by

   - snapping a photo or video of you reading aloud
   - challenging three of your friends to join the fun
   - sharing to Twitter or Instagram using the hashtags #WRADChallenge and #WorldReadAloudDay

#StoryIs

"Story is the unique way we connect and relate to the people in our everyday lives."

TINA ATHAIDE, AUTHOR OF *MEENA'S MINDFUL MOMENT*

Poem in Your Pocket Day

If you're a lover of poetry, you already know the unending stories that can be found in this powerful format. I love how a small poem tells a whole story, how that story resonates long after you finish the poem, and how, when you connect deeply with a poem, you immediately want to share that connection with everyone you see. Poem in Your Pocket Day started in New York City in 2002. In 2008, the Academy of American Poets encouraged everyone to participate. It's one of the best days of the year, and it's easy to celebrate. On this day, which is always in April during National Poetry Month, find a poem or write a poem and put it in your pocket. Wear a sticker that says, "Ask me about my poem." Anyone on a campus can participate in this celebration of poetry—students, bus drivers, cafeteria workers, school secretaries, librarians, music teachers, gym teachers, classroom teachers—everyone!

If you're musically inclined, you may want to introduce Poem in Your Pocket Day by playing Emily Arrow's "Poem in Your Pocket" song (linked in QR code below). This catchy tune is included on Emily's Storytime Singalong, Volume 1 *and on her YouTube channel. There's sheet music if you want to play along, and if you like to move with the music, you'll also find the motion guide she created to go with the tune!*

"Poem in Your Pocket"
by Emily Arrow (2016), from
Storytime Singalong, Volume 1

This collection of picture books will help you grow Poem in Your Pocket Day.

- ♥ *A Pocketful of Poems* by Nikki Grimes (2001); illustrated by Javaka Steptoe

- ♥ *Pocket Poems* by Bobbi Katz (2004); illustrated by Marilyn Hafner

- ♥ *More Pocket Poems* by Bobbi Katz (2009); illustrated by Deborah Zemke

- ♥ *Poem in Your Pocket for Young Poets* by Bruno Navasky (2011)

- ♥ *A Poem in Your Pocket* by Margaret McNamara (2015); illustrated by G. Brian Karas

- ♥ *Keep a Pocket in Your Poem: Classic Poems and Playful Parodies* by J. Patrick Lewis (2017); illustrated by Johanna Wright

- ♥ *Poem in My Pocket* by Chris Tougas (2021); illustrated by Josée Bisaillon

- ♥ *If This Bird Had Pockets: A Poem in Your Pocket Day Celebration* by Amy Ludwig Vanderwater (2022); illustrated by Emma J. Virján

#StoryIs

"Story is what connects me and you. It's my grandmother Nana's voice over dinner where years later you can't remember the food, but you remember the taste of her stories."

REEM FARUQI, AUTHOR OF UNSETTLED

Picture Book Month

I love picture books. I collect them. I share them. I write them. Our students are never too old to be read aloud a picture book or to read aloud a picture book. Too often, as young readers move toward the upper grades, they're discouraged from checking out and reading picture books. This is both unfortunate and ironic because this is the exact same time when they can finally read them independently. The founders of Picture Book Month encourage us to read, share, and celebrate a picture book every day during November—with children of all ages.

I asked teacher-librarian and Picture Book Month champion Margie Myers-Culver to share her thoughts on picture books and how reading communities can connect through them during Picture Book Month.

"Picture books connect the written word to the world."

DEBORAH FREEDMAN

"Picture books are one of my favorite things in the world. I love the marriage of word and art, each making the other better. They teach us something at every age."

TRACI SORELL

Margie Myers-Culver

I hold great affection for picture books. These worlds generated from imaginations and gathered from information have always been and always will be a part of both my professional and personal collections. They have no equal as a read-aloud. I have watched listeners, whatever age they are, sit in total stunned silence. I've seen their eyes fill with tears. I've heard their sighs, gasps, and bursts of laughter. These narratives reach out, finding common ground within listeners and readers, supplying connections we will remember and store in our collective hearts.

There is power in picture books. The carefully chosen words and the pictorial interpretation of those words in art, using a range of color, mediums, techniques and styles, layouts and designs, connect with readers on an emotional level no one can predict because we bring our own personal experiences to each book. Of this truth, author-illustrator John Hendrix (2021) says in the author's note at the close of *Go and Do Likewise!*, "In the mysterious canvas of our hearts and minds, stories, word pictures, and vivid ideas create a deep pool of wonder and understanding."

For this reason, one of the most successful Picture Book Month activities is a school-wide annual Mock Caldecott. To begin, we display past Caldecott Medal winners, arranged with a placard designating the type of medium used. If you want to get a jump start, you and your students can collect possible Caldecott nominees throughout the year and store them on a Padlet board. Then, when The Horn Book's (2021) "Calling Caldecott" blog series begins posting nominees in September, you can have fun comparing your group's titles with the official selections.

After the nominees are announced, in September, we spend about four or five weeks discussing the illustrations in the selected titles, the style and medium used by the illustrators, and how the images work with the text or sometimes without text. We review the five items listed under the criteria at the Association for Library Service to Children's (2021) Caldecott Medal page. We look for details. We try to understand what the illustrator is conveying to readers. We talk about our initial reaction to each book and how we feel about it after closer examination.

To cast their vote, each student is given a ballot, which includes a picture of each book's front cover, the title, the author's and illustrator's names, the medium used, and a place for notes. The students cast their votes for the winner, and then we name the runners-up as honor books. For additional fun, you can lead a class-by-class comparison or a whole-school tally, or you might even consider merging your Mock Caldecott contest with another class or with another campus.

The value of picture books to connect readers of all ages, regardless of the intended audience, was never more apparent than during the last two months of my ninety-four-year-old mom's life. Every day I would read her at least one picture book. On the last evening I spent with her, when I arrived in her room, she was lightly sleeping. When she realized I was there and saw the three picture books I was holding, her entire demeanor changed. For the time I spent reading those stories with her, she was lively, filled with smiles and laughter. We chatted about how children would feel about those books. Whether planned or impromptu, whether you are a third-grade student discussing a picture book during a Mock Caldecott unit or a mother listening to your daughter read aloud a picture book, the same daughter you spun tales for to get her to eat lunch, stories connect us throughout our lives.

ALA Youth Media Awards

You can replicate or extend this Mock Caldecott process with other popular book awards. Check out the various ALA Youth Media Awards at ALA.org, explore their selection criteria, and you're on your way to making them come to life in your classroom or library!

- ♥ Coretta Scott King Awards—Named after author, activist, and civil rights leader Coretta Scott King and awarded annually since 1970, these prestigious awards are given to the authors and illustrators of books for children and young adults that show an appreciation of African American culture and universal human values.

- ♥ Newbery Medal—Awarded annually since 1922 and named after British bookseller John Newbery, this award is given to the author of the most *distinguished* contribution to children's literature for children up to age fourteen.

- ♥ Pura Belpré Awards—Named after children's librarian Pura Belpré, these awards are given to a Latino/Latina author and illustrator that authentically shows and celebrates the Latino cultural experience in books for children and young adults.

- ♥ Schneider Family Book Awards—In 2003, Dr. Katherine Schneider endowed this award for books that show an artistic expression of the disability experience for young readers.

- ♥ Sibert Informational Book Medal—Named after Robert F. Sibert, the former president of Bound to Stay Bound Books, this award is given to the author(s) and illustrator(s) of the most distinguished informational book for children.

- ♥ Stonewall Book Awards—Given for the first time in 1971, these awards honor exceptional books about the LGBTQIA+ experience.

Mr. Schu Suggests

As I mentioned earlier, you'll notice considerable overlap among the affective elements of story discussed across this book and this is especially true in this chapter. Since story as connector threads across every discussion we've had along the way, this list of suggestions—perhaps more than any other—will reflect this beautiful reciprocity. This is the ultimate gift of story, meeting us where we are, just when we need it most, inviting us to self-select into what the experience means for us.

 *Hair Twins* by Raakhee Mirchandani; illustrated by Holly Hatam

Hair Twins is the story of a young Sikh girl and the bond she and her father share over their hair. You see how the daily ritual of fixing their hair together adds joy and a deep connection to their lives. Raakhee wrote this story based on her relationship with her father and her daughter's relationship with her husband. She hopes readers feel connected to their relationship and inspired to share their own traditions.

APPLICATION TO STORY AS CONNECTOR

Just as the shared ritual of doing their hair connects the father and daughter, shared rituals connect us as well. Students can talk about a shared ritual they have and discuss the people it connects them to.

 *Nicky & Vera: A Quiet Hero of the Holocaust and the Children He Rescued* by Peter Sís

This poignant picture book is the true story of Nicholas Winton and Vera Gissing. Instead of taking a ski trip, Nicholas went to Prague at the request of a friend, where he ended up working to help evacuate, and ultimately save, 669 children shortly before WWII began. Vera is one of these children. Their stories, which remained untold for many years, are entwined in the pages of this story. The author's note explains how he happened upon this story as well as his connection to it.

APPLICATION TO STORY AS CONNECTOR

Peter Sís's haunting illustrations illuminate the connection we have with our past. As the children board the train, Peter illustrates their bodies as full of the things they are leaving behind. When he illustrates Nicky leaving the war and moving on with his life, he shows his body with all the events, up to that point, that made Nicky the person he was. When he illustrates the adults that, as children, were saved by Nicky, you see that younger child inside of every illustration of their grown selves. This story, and these illustrations, will foster powerful discussions about how the person we are today is connected to events in our past.

What Lane? by Torrey Maldonado

In *What Lane?*, Stephen, a biracial sixth grader, grows up hanging out with his friends and feeling as though they can do anything together until the day he gets treated differently from his friends— even though they all made the same mistake. This is when Stephen starts to realize how his race impacts others' perceptions of him. He starts to question if he really can do it all or if "lanes" exist that he must navigate through. Stephen's new awareness of the Black Lives Matter movement leads to further questions as he works to determine how to navigate through his friendships while defining his own way.

In a recent interview with the author, I asked him to share something Stephen, the main character, would want me to ask if I were interviewing him instead. He responded with, "So, you asking your question is you saying, 'Stephen, your voice matters. Show me what *you* want me to know.' That's you offering him lanes and asking, 'What lane?' If you do that, you'd be like his allies of the book. He'd smile big and lean in because he'd feel your empathy. He'd take his foot off the brake society presses on his heart and he'd put his foot on the pedal of sharing, and you'd both drive to a higher ground of empathy and alliance" (Maldonado 2020).

This book is a conversation starter and a conversation expander. It helps us connect because it highlights what happens when we stay in our comfort zone and don't branch out. Students who read it learn the importance of creating friendships with others who they may feel are different than themselves. It also helps students connect as they further consider movements such as Black Lives Matter and how coming together as humans helps us ultimately create a world that is better for everyone.

Hello, Earth! Poems to Our Planet by Joyce Sidman; illustrated by Miren Asiain Lora

In this book of poems, the narrator questions the Earth in an attempt to uncover its secrets. It speaks to Earth as though it were a living being, and acknowledges that it is. It also addresses our connection to the earth and the impact our actions have.

APPLICATION TO STORY AS CONNECTOR

Joyce Sidman explicitly acknowledges the connection we have with the Earth when she says, "We are connected. In taking care of you, we take care of ourselves." Resources at the end of the book assist the reader in learning more about climate change and how to help the environment This is an excellent selection for Earth Day or when talking about the importance of caring for our planet. Students can identify how their actions impact the Earth and come up with concrete ideas to lessen the damage we do to it.

Swashby and the Sea by Beth Ferry; illustrated by Juana Martinez-Neal

This book tells the gentle story of a cantankerous man who lives by the sea and is content living an isolated life without the intrusion of others. A young girl and her grandmother move in next door and try to make friends with him, but, despite their best attempts, he pushes them away. The sea, however, has other plans for Swashby and his new neighbors.

Teacher-librarian Donna Kouri chose this title as her campus's One Book, One School selection because it shows the importance of connection and how people who may appear to prefer isolation will gravitate toward others when the time is right. After reading this, students may feel moved to reach out and connect with those in need of a connection, such as seniors living alone in a nursing home.

Sunday Funday in Koreatown by Aram Kim

Yoomi loves Sunday Funday. It's a day filled with her favorite things. One Sunday, Yoomi's Sunday Funday is filled with mishaps that threaten to ruin her day until she realizes that, although it isn't perfect, it can still be a fun day after all.

Aram shared with me she wrote this story based on her own childhood memory of taking long walks with her dad on Sundays around town, to the library, and to her grandma's house. She said, "After my dad passed away in 2012, writing and drawing a story based on my memory with him helped me cope with the loss and to commemorate him" (Kim 2021).

APPLICATION TO STORY AS CONNECTOR

Yoomi mistakenly connects material objects as the key to fun—her favorite show, her favorite shirt, her favorite food. Ultimately, the connection she shares with her grandmother and the love they share help put her day back on the right track, turning it into a true Sunday Funday. We all have a connection with someone who makes our bad days seem better. Students can discuss someone who helps them feel better when things seem terrible.

Bear Is a Bear by Jonathan Stutzman; illustrated by Dan Santat

Bear Is a Bear shows the friendship between a stuffed bear and its owner. The friendship grows from that of uncertainty, to deep companionship, to increased independence, to new beginnings.

When I asked Jonathan what a bear means to him, he responded with, "A bear is a bear that reminds me of the love, warmth, laughter (tickles!), and absolute safety I felt as a child, in my mother's arms" (Stutzman 2021).

APPLICATION TO STORY AS CONNECTOR

This book highlights the uncertainty and rocky roads that often accompany new friendships. It encourages children to give each other a chance and not to immediately judge a person and their potential to be a true companion. It shows connections can be difficult at first, change over time, but can last forever.

Where Three Oceans Meet by Rajani LaRocca; illustrated by Archana Sreenivasan

Sejal and her mother are visiting her Pati in India as they prepare to take a trip to the bottom of India where the three oceans meet. Sejal becomes sick on the journey. As she dozes off, she hears the stories her Pati and mother are saying and realizes that as strong as they are as individuals, they are even stronger together. The idea for this story came to Dr. Rajani LaRocca during a conversation she had where she described a trip she took to Kanyakumari, the spot where the Indian Ocean, the Arabian Sea, and the Bay of Bengal meet. She shared the following with me: "I found myself writing a story about a girl who makes that trip with her mother and grandmother, and what she discovers along the way. I wanted to convey how, although we often think about our destinations, it's often the small moments during a journey— especially the moments we share with those we love—that mean the most" (LaRocca 2021).

This story shows connection in so many ways. It shows how we remain connected even when apart, how food brings us together, and how even the land offers connections. It's evident throughout the story that connections create strength. Classrooms can explore these connections and talk about foods meaningful to their families or how they connect with family and friends that may be far away.

🌀 *Seven Special Somethings: A Nowruz Story* by Adib Khorram; illustrated by Zainab Faidhi

Kian is excited to celebrate the Persian New Year holiday of Nowruz with his family, but in his excitement, he upsets the sofreh haft-seen and all its symbolic items. Determined to make this New Year as happy as possible, he scours the house looking for seven new symbols, all which must begin with the letter S. With some ingenuity, Kian creates a unique sofreh haft-seen that represents his family and ensures a happy new year.

APPLICATION TO STORY AS CONNECTOR

Kian is connected to his family and Norwruz. In the same way Kian finds symbols representing his family, invite students to share symbols that are meaningful in their lives and to reflect on a time they gathered with family or friends to wish happiness for others. As Adib mentions in his author's note, "At its heart, Nowruz isn't about tables, or S's, or food. It's about gathering together with the people you love to wish for happiness in the coming year."

🌀 *Mañanaland* by Pam Muñoz Ryan

Maximiliano Feliciano Esteban Cordoba is being raised by his father and yearns to know more about his mother. He grows up immersed in stories and legends shared by his father and his beloved Buelo, especially the legends of the gatekeepers. Desperate to learn more about his mother, Max uncovers a secret that may lead him to her, or at least to discover more information about her. While his father is away, Max secretly follows this lead and finds himself living the legend, a legend far more dangerous and important than he ever could have imagined. As Pam Muñoz Ryan (2019) points out, "His story could have happened decades ago, it is happening now, and it will likely continue in the tomorrows to come."

APPLICATION TO STORY AS CONNECTOR

Mañanaland is an outstanding read-aloud and the perfect book club selection to engage readers' hearts. Compelling and beautifully written, it lends itself to meaningful and important discussions about goodwill and perseverance and how we shouldn't rush to judgment until we know all the facts. Most of all, it is a compassion-building story, one that will connect students to each other and to those facing similar situations.

Our Table by Peter H. Reynolds

Violet has fond memories of the time she and her family spent around a beloved table. As time passes, she finds the table empty as her family becomes engrossed in television, cell phones, and video games. Rather than making memories together, they are off on their own connecting with others through electronics. This breaks Violet's heart. She decides to take action and comes up with a plan to bring them together again while, at the same time, meeting them where they are.

APPLICATION TO STORY AS CONNECTOR

This is a perfect lesson to pair with digital citizenship lessons. As Peter H. Reynolds (2020) eloquently states, "We must remember, as we squeeze through the portal of the future, that we bring with us what we know works, what is most important. Human connection. Shared stories. Shared memories." Students see how excessive use of technology, of any kind, can impede personal connections, and that with some reflective guidelines, we can still enjoy technology while at the same time connecting in person with those around us.

My favorite titles for story as connector

The Story Continues...

D o you feel a deep connection to a specific place or spot? Maybe it's when you're reading a book or people-watching while sitting on your favorite bench, the one near the humongous sycamore tree in your neighborhood park. Or perhaps it's when you stop by a local bakery, the one with the most delicious and mouthwatering blueberry scones with lemon glaze you've ever tasted. Or possibly it's when you're browsing the shelves inside a two-story independent bookshop, the one that smells like home to your heart. For me? It's when I'm in New York City! It's where I go to recharge and to connect with the sites, the sounds, the theaters, the people. And it's where I met a wonderful family in an encounter I'll never forget.

Let's back up a bit.

I headed to LaGuardia Airport after three wonderful and rejuvenating Days of John (D.O.J. for short). Jeremy Fink inspired this tradition. In Wendy Mass's (2008) middle-grade novel, *Jeremy Fink and the Meaning of Life,* Jeremy names the time between 11:00 p.m. and 12:00 a.m. as the Hour of Jeremy (H.O.J. for short). During this daily ritual, he reads from the books on his shelf (including at least fifteen minutes on time travel), researches topics he's interested in, and eats peanut butter. He loves this time of day because the world feels calm and asleep. This inspired me as a teacher-librarian who often forgot to take time for myself. By taking time for myself, I was a better teacher and advocate for my students.

Feeling rejuvenated and ready to return to school after a wonderful spring break full of D.O.J. time, I arrived at the airport and immediately learned my flight was canceled. The next available flight wasn't for two days. I found myself standing in an extremely long line with angry passengers. Everyone in the ticketing area was on edge. A mother and her two children were in line behind me. Understandably, as we waited and waited and waited, the children became increasingly less patient. They started arguing with each other. Kicking their suitcases. Their mother was patient and loving, but obviously exasperated, as she tried to keep them calm while booking a rental car by phone for what would end up being an unplanned 830-mile drive home.

As I thought about ways I might help, my mind floated back to the comfort books always give me in situations where I'm feeling unsettled or anxious. How they calm me and how they center me. How they take me away. By now, you know that I'm never without a book, and, in the way stories seem to find the perfect reader at the perfect time, I knew *If You Find This* (Baker 2015) would speak to these children. I'd packed it away in hopes of reading it on the flight home, but I could sense their hearts yearning for this story. They needed it more than I did.

Weeks later, a letter arrived in the mail.

Dear Mr. Schu,

Hi! We met in LaGuardia Airport when our flight was canceled. I hope you had a good trip home. We drove home. It was a LONG ride, but I had the book you gave me to read. If You Find This is an amazing book! Thank you so much for giving it to me. I hope you get a chance to read it too. I'm not done with it yet, but it is so good and funny and emotional. Thank you for talking with me at the airport. You made a scary time fun, and the book made a boring drive interesting.

This is what story does. It connects us. It gives us calm in the storms of life. It rejuvenates us. It helps us feel safe. Reading someone else's story can inspire us to tell our own stories and live our authentic life. Stories contain the healing power to make our hearts calmer and more compassionate, comfortable, and roomy. In my favorite scene from *Flora and Ulysses: The Illuminated Adventures* (DiCamillo 2013), Dr. Meescham describes this type of openheartedness with the perfect word—*capacious*. When our hearts are capacious, they are bigger and fuller, and they guide us to connect, empathize, and heal—they're enormously "capable of containing" so much more than we ever imagined.

Together, let's make hearts more capacious. Together, let's share the gift of story by cultivating effective, positive experiences through the act of reading—for the readers we teach and reach, for the learning communities we serve and care about, and for ourselves.

Together, let's share our hearts through story.

Acknowledgments

Dear Books 🖤 You wrapped your arms around me as I wrote. You inspire, heal wounds, clarify big questions about the world, encourage me to move feelings to action, and connect me with and to something bigger than myself. You helped me feel less alone as a child. You provided comfort as I struggled with disordered eating and when I questioned my self-worth in middle and high school. You made me a better classroom teacher, teacher-librarian, and human. Thanks to you, I'm a card catalog of stories.

Dear Universe 🖤 Ten years from now, when I reflect on writing this book, the actual typing of every paragraph and each chapter will be associated with a specific place and time. Connected to a smile, a mood, a trying time, and a generous gesture, such as airplanes, hotel rooms around the world, joy walks, my cat, Lou Grant, knocking notebooks and pens off a table, long weekends at Terry and Jeff's writing retreat, a global pandemic, and New York City. Oh, NYC! Your energy, your parks, your restaurants (hello to Phil at Junior's on 45th Street), and your theaters. You reenergize me. I'm grateful, eternally.

Dear Michael Cunningham 🖤 Thank you for writing *The Hours*. One day I'll write about how it had a huge and lasting impact on me during college. Thank you for introducing me to Mrs. Dalloway!

Dear Dr. Mary Margaret Reed 🖤 Thank you for inspiring and motivating me in the fifth grade. Thank you for introducing me to characters and stories that have stayed with me for more than thirty years.

Dear Alanis Morrissette, Adrienne Warren, Ben Platt, Cynthia Erivo, Josh Groban, Jonathan Groff, André De Shields, Ani DiFranco, Natalie Merchant, Mandy Gonzalez, Miriam-Teak Lee, Sara Bareilles, and the Entire Original Broadway Cast of *Waitress: The Musical* 🖤 Your ability to share stories through music inspires me. Thank you for singing songs I listened to on repeat as I wrote and revised this book.

Dear Jennifer LaGarde 💜 Your *fRUday* text messages (around 9:00 p.m. CT every Friday) were the best. Thank you for making me laugh and smile.

Dear Robin Hoffman, Donalyn Miller, Deborah Roberts, and Anne Wissinger 💜 Our work together on the Scholastic Reading Summits filled my heart with warm fuzzies and sunshine. Thank you for building something so important, valuable, and student focused.

Dear Kate DiCamillo 💜 Thank you for always checking in on the status of my heart. Thank you for reminding me the only way out is through and for encouraging me to bring my heart to the page, just like I do to the stage. Thank you for helping me better understand my heart. You are, as you write in *Francine Poulet Meets the Ghost Raccoon* (2015), the genuine article.

Dear Kelly Yang, Maulik Pancholy, Donna Kouri, Rhonda Jenkins, Debbie Ridpath Ohi, Dr. Karen Biggs-Tucker, Dr. Brian Tucker, Deirdre Iuliani, Kelly Gustafson, Dr. LaQuita Outlaw, and Margie Myers-Culver 💜 I'm sending you a humongous and heartfelt thank-you for sharing your wisdom in this book. Thank you for caring about your readers' and students' hearts.

Dear Katherine Applegate 💜 Thank you for your generous foreword. Thank you for writing books that help readers open their hearts. Thank you for your friendship.

Dear Students and Colleagues in Seoul, Kankakee, Oswego, Oak Brook, and at Rutgers University 💜 You'll always have a special place in my heart. Thank you for sharing the books of your hearts with me.

Dear Students, Educators, and Administrators I Met as the Ambassador of School Libraries for Scholastic Book Fairs 💜 Thank you for inviting me to your schools to celebrate stories and reading. Thank you for heart-growing and life-changing experiences.

Dear Mom, Bobby, Lisa, Addison, and Evelynn 💜 Words fail me. Thank you for beginnings, for books, and for encouragement. I am who I am today because of you.

Dear Paul 💜 Thank you for supporting me and believing in me. You are home to me in so many ways.

Dear Shannon St. Peter, Lynne Costa, Cindy Butler, and Gina Poirier 💜 Your work on this book of my heart has touched my heart in more ways than you could know. Thank you for loving this project as much as I have.

Dear Terry 💜 I could write an entire chapter about you and your generous heart. Thank you for your patience, guidance, and generous feedback. Thank you for listening to me as I went on and on and on for fifteen minutes about an idea, which you then helped me shape and share in one or two sentences. Thank you for going on this journey through story together. Thank you for believing in me and for providing this space.

Dear Reader 💜 Thank you for reading these words of my heart. Thank you for sharing your heart through story. Thank you for showing your students the healing love and hope stories can provide.

Love,

John Sch

Children's Literature Bibliography

Agell, Charlotte. 2019. *Maybe Tomorrow?* Illustrated by Ana Ramírez González. New York: Scholastic.

Ahmed, Samira. 2018. *Love, Hate & Other Filters.* New York: Soho Teen.

———. 2019. *Internment.* New York: Little, Brown Books for Young Readers.

———. 2021. *Amira and Hamza: The War to Save the Worlds.* New York: Little, Brown Books for Young Readers

Anderson, John David. 2017. *Ms. Bixby's Last Day.* New York: Walden Pond.

Angleberger, Tom. 2010. *The Strange Case of Origami Yoda.* New York: Abrams Books for Young Readers.

Applegate, Katherine. 2012. *The One and Only Ivan.* New York: HarperCollins.

———. 2015. *Crenshaw.* New York: Feiwel and Friends.

———. 2020. *The One and Only Bob.* HarperCollins.

Arrow, Emily. 2016. "Poem in Your Pocket." Recorded on February 5, 2016, track 9 on *Storytime Singalong, Volume 1*, compact disc.

Athaide, Tina. 2021. *Meena's Mindful Moment.* Illustrated by Åsa Gilland. Salem, MA: Page Street Kids.

Baker, Matthew. 2015. *If You Find This.* New York: Little, Brown Books for Young Readers.

Baptiste, Tracey. 2018. *Minecraft: The Crash.* New York: Del Ray Books.

Barnes, Derrick. 2020. *I Am Every Good Thing.* Illustrated by Gordon C. James. New York: Nancy Paulsen Books.

Barnett, Mac. 2019. *The Important Thing About Margaret Wise Brown.* Illustrated by Sarah Jacoby. New York: Balzer + Bray.

Barnhill, Kelly. 2016. *The Girl Who Drank the Moon.* New York: Algonquin Young Readers.

Baron, Chris. 2021. *The Magical Imperfect.* New York: Feiwel and Friends.

Bell, Cece. 2014. *El Deafo*. New York: Amulet Books.

Bildner, Phil. 2020. *A High Five for Glenn Burke*. New York: Farrar, Straus and Giroux.

Blake, Ashley Herring. 2018. *Ivy Aberdeen's Letter to the World*. Little, Brown Books for Young Readers.

Blume, Judy. 1970. *Are You There God? It's Me, Margaret*. New York: Simon and Schuster.

Braden, Ann. 2018. *The Benefits of Being an Octopus*. New York: Sky Pony.

————. 2021. *Flight of the Puffin*. New York: Nancy Paulsen Books.

Bradley, Kimberly Brubaker. 2020. *Fighting Words*. New York: Dial Books.

Burach, Ross. 2021. *The Little Butterfly That Could*. New York: Scholastic.

Cassie, Aiden. 2020. *The Word for Friend*. New York: Farrar, Straus and Giroux.

Castillo, Lauren. 2020. *Our Friend Hedgehog: The Story of Us*. New York: Alfred A. Knopf Books for Young Readers.

Charles, Tami. 2019. *Freedom Soup*. Illustrated by Jacqueline Alcántara. Somerville, MA: Candlewick.

Cisneros, Ernesto. 2020. *Efrén Divided*. New York: Quill Tree Books.

Cole, Henry. 2020. *One Little Bag*. New York: Scholastic.

Cordell, Matthew. 2020. *Hello, Neighbor: The Kind and Caring World of Mister Rogers*. New York: Neal Porter Books.

Craft, Jerry. 2020. *Class Act*. New York: Quill Tree Books.

Creech, Sharon. 2001. *A Fine, Fine School*. Illustrated by Harry Bliss. New York: HarperCollins.

————. 2003. *Granny Torrelli Makes Soup*. New York: HarperCollins.

Cuevas, Adrianna. 2021. *Cuba in My Pocket*. New York: Farrar, Straus and Giroux.

DasGupta, Sayantani. 2018. *The Serpent's Secret*. Kiranmala and the Kingdom Beyond, Book 1. New York: Scholastic.

————. 2021. *Force of Fire*. New York: Scholastic.

Dias, Marley. 2018. *Marley Dias Gets It Done: And So Can You*. New York: Scholastic.

DiCamillo, Kate. 2013. *Flora and Ulysses: The Illuminated Adventures*. Illustrated by K.G. Campbell. Somerville, MA: Candlewick.

————. 2015. *Francine Poulet Meets the Ghost Raccoon*. Illustrated by Chris Van Dusen. Somerville, MA: Candlewick.

———. 2018. *Louisiana's Way Home*. Somerville, MA: Candlewick.

———. 2019. *A Piglet Named Mercy*. Somerville, MA: Candlewick.

Doerrfeld, Cori. 2018. *The Rabbit Listened*. New York: Dial Books.

Elliott, Zetta. 2020. *A Place Inside of Me: A Poem to Heal the Heart*. Illustrated by Noa Denmon. New York: Farrar, Straus and Giroux.

Engle, Margarita. 2019. *Dancing Hands: How Teresa Carreño Played the Piano for President Lincoln*. Illustrated by Rafael López. New York: Atheneum Books for Young Readers.

Faruqi, Reem. 2021. *Unsettled*. New York: HarperCollins.

Faruqi, Saadia. 2021. *Yusuf Azeem Is Not a Hero*. New York: Quill Tree Books.

Federle, Tim. 2013. *Better Nate Than Ever*. New York: Simon and Schuster.

Ferry, Beth. 2020. *Swashy and the Sea*. Illustrated by Juana Martinez-Neal. Boston: HMH Books for Young Readers.

Fipps, Lisa. 2021. *Starfish*. New York: Nancy Paulsen Books.

Fleming, Candace. 2020. *Honeybee: The Busy Life of* Apis Mellifera. Illustrated by Eric Rohmann. New York: Neal Porter Books.

Florence, Debbie Michiko. 2020. *Keep It Together, Keiko Carter*. New York: Scholastic.

Fogliano, Julie. *My Best Friend*. Illustrated by Jillian Tamaki. New York: Atheneum Books for Young Readers.

Freedman, Deborah. 2019. *Carl and the Meaning of Life*. New York: Viking Books for Young Readers.

———. 2021. *Is Was*. New York: Atheneum Books for Young Readers.

Gertler, Caroline. 2021. *Many Points of Me*. New York: Greenwillow Books.

Glaser, Karina Yan. 2021. *The Vanderbeekers Make a Wish*. Boston, HMH Books for Young Readers.

Grimes, Nikki. 2001. *A Pocketful of Poems*. Illustrated by Javaka Steptoe. Boston: Clarion Books.

———. 2019. *Ordinary Hazards: A Memoir*. New York: WordSong.

———. 2020. *Kamala Harris: Rooted in Justice*. Illustrated by Laura Freeman. New York: Atheneum Books for Young Readers.

Hagan, Ellen. 2021. *Reckless, Glorious, Girl*. New York: Bloomsbury Children's Books.

Heidicker, Christian McKay. 2021. *Scary Stories for Young Foxes: The City*. New York: Henry Holt and Co. Books for Young Readers.

Henderson, Leah. 2021. *A Day for Rememberin': Inspired by the True Events of the First Memorial Day*. Illustrated by Floyd Cooper. New York: Abrams Books for Young Readers.

Hendrix, John. 2021. *Go and Do Likewise!* New York: Abrams Books for Young Readers.

Henkes, Kevin. 1996. *Lilly's Purple Plastic Purse*. New York: Greenwillow Books.

———. 2000. *Wemberly Worried*. New York: Greenwillow Books.

———. 2013. *The Year of Billy Miller*. New York: Greenwillow Books.

———. 2015. *Waiting*. New York: Greenwillow Books.

Hesse, Karen. 1997. *Out of the Dust*. New York: Scholastic.

Hiranandani, Veera. 2018. *The Night Diary*. New York: Kokila.

Hood, Susan, and Pathana Sornhiran. 2019. *Titan and the Wild Boars: The True Cave Rescue of the Thai Soccer Team*. Illustrated by Dow Phumiruk. New York: HarperCollins.

Hubbard, Rita Lorraine. 2020. *The Oldest Student: How Mary Walker Learned to Read*. Illustrated by Oge Mora. New York: Schwartz and Wade.

Hunt, Lynda Mullaly. 2015. *Fish in a Tree*. New York: Nancy Paulsen Books.

Jacobson, Darlene Beck. 2020. *Wishes, Dares, and How to Stand Up to a Bully*. Berkeley, CA: Creston Books.

Jamieson, Victoria, and Omar Mohamed. 2020. *When Stars Are Scattered*. New York: Dial Books.

Johnson, Varian. 2020. *Twins*. Illustrated by Shannon Wright. New York: Graphix.

Katz, Bobbi. 2004. *Pocket Poems*. Illustrated by Marilyn Hafner. New York: Dutton Books for Young Readers.

———. 2009. *More Pocket Poems*. Illustrated by Deborah Zemke. New York: Dutton Books for Young Readers.

Kelkar, Supriya. 2019. *The Many Colors of Harpreet Singh*. Illustrated by Alea Marley. New York: Sterling Children's Books.

———. 2021. *That Thing About Bollywood*. New York: Simon and Schuster Books for Young Readers.

Kelly, Erin Entrada. 2021. *Maybe Maybe Marisol Rainey*. New York: Greenwillow Books.

Kelly, Lynne. 2019. *Song for a Whale*. New York: Delacorte Books for Young Readers.

Khorram, Adib. 2021. *Seven Special Somethings: A Nowruz Story*. Illustrated by Zainab Faidhi. New York: Dial Books.

Kim, Aram. 2021. *Sunday Funday in Koreatown*. New York: Holiday House.

Klise, Kate. 2017. *Stay: A Girl, a Dog, a Bucket List*. Illustrated by M. Sarah Klise. New York: Feiwel and Friends.

Knowles, Jo. 2022. *Ear Worm*. Illustrated by Galia Bernstein. Somerville, MA: Candlewick.

Lackey, Lindsay. 2019. *All the Impossible Things*. New York: Roaring Brook.

Lai, Thanhhà. 2016. *Listen, Slowly*. New York: HarperCollins.

LaRocca, Rajani. 2021a. *Red, White, and Whole*. New York: Quill Tree Books.

———. 2021b. *Where Three Oceans Meet*. Illustrated by Archana Sreenivasan. New York: Abrams Books for Young Readers.

Lê, Minh. 2020. *Lift*. Illustrated by Dan Santat. New York: Little, Brown Books for Young Readers.

Levinson, Cynthia. 2021. *The People's Painter: How Ben Shahn Fought for Justice with Art*. Illustrated by Evan Turk. New York: Abrams Books for Young Readers.

Levis, Caron. 2016. *Ida, Always*. Illustrated by Charles Santoso. New York: Abrams Books for Young Readers.

———. 2020. *This Way, Charlie*. Illustrated by Charles Santoso. New York: Abrams Books for Young Readers.

Lewis, Patrick J. 2017. *Keep a Pocket in Your Poem: Classic Poems and Playful Parodies*. Illustrated by Johanna Wright. New York: Wordsong.

Lindstrom, Carole. 2020. *We Are Water Protectors*. Illustrated by Michaela Goade. New York: Roaring Brook.

Lloyd, Megan Wagner. 2021. *Allergic*. Illustrated by Megan Mee Nutter. New York: Graphix.

London, Jonathan. 2004. *The Eyes of Gray Wolf*. Illustrated by Jon Van Zyle. San Francisco: Chronicle Books.

Lucianovic, Stephanie V. W. 2019. *The End of Something Wonderful: A Practical Guide to a Backyard Funeral*. Illustrated by George Ermos. New York: Sterling Children's Books.

Lucido, Aimee. 2019. *Emmy in the Key of Code*. Boston: Versify Books.

Ludwig, Trudy. 2020. *The Power of One: Every Act of Kindness Counts*. Illustrated by Mike Curato. Alfred A. Knopf Books for Young Readers.

Luyken, Corinna. 2019. *My Heart*. New York: Dial Books.

Maillard, Kevin Noble. 2019. *Fry Bread: A Native American Family Story*. Illustrated by Juana Martinez-Neal. New York: Roaring Brook.

Maldonado, Torrey. 2020 *What Lane?* New York: Nancy Paulsen Books.

Mass, Wendy. 2008. *Jeremy Fink and the Meaning of Life*. New York: Little, Brown Books for Young Readers.

McGhee, Holly M. 2017. *Come with Me*. Illustrated by Pascal Lemaître. New York: G.P. Putnam's Sons.

McNamara, Margaret. 2011. *A Poem in Your Pocket*. Illustrated by G. Brian Karas. New York: Schwartz and Wade.

Medina, Meg. 2021. *Merci Suárez Can't Dance*. Somerville, MA: Candlewick.

Messner, Kate. 2020. *The Next President. The Unexpected Beginnings and Unwritten Future of America's Presidents*. Illustrated by Adam Rex. San Francisco: Chronicle Books.

———. 2020–2021. History Smashers series. New York: Random House Books for Young Readers.

Mirchandani, Raakhee. 2021. *Hair Twins*. Illustrated by Holly Hatam. New York: Little, Brown Books for Young Readers.

Mora, Oge. 2019. *Saturday*. New York: Little, Brown Books for Young Readers.

Morales, Yuyi. 2019. *Dreamers*. New York: Neal Porter Books.

Morris, Richard T. 2019. *Bear Came Along*. Illustrated by LeUyen Pham. New York: Little, Brown Books for Young Readers.

Moundlic, Charlotte. 2009. *The Scar*. Illustrated by Olivier Tallec. Somerville, MA: Candlewick.

Myers, Walter Dean. 1999. *Monster*. New York: HarperCollins.

Navasky, Bruno. 2011. *Poem in Your Pocket for Young Poets*. New York: Abrams Books for Young Readers.

Ness, Patrick. 2011. *A Monster Calls*. Somerville, MA: Candlewick.

Noel, Kaela. 2020. *Coo*. New York: Greenwillow Books.

Nyong'O, Lupita. 2019. *Sulwe*. Illustrated by Vashti Harrison. New York: Simon and Schuster Books for Young Readers.

Ohi, Debbie Ridpath. 2017. *Sam & Eva*. New York: Simon and Schuster Books for Young Readers.

Palacio, R. J. 2012. *Wonder*. New York: Knopf Books for Young Readers.

Pancholy, Maulik. 2019. *The Best at It*. New York: Balzer + Bray.

Park, Linda Sue. 2001. *A Single Shard*. Boston: HMH Books for Young Readers.

———. 2020. *Gurple and Preen: A Broken Crayon Cosmic Adventure*. Illustrated by Debbie Ridpath Ohi. New York: Simon and Schuster.

Patterson, Katherine. 1977. *Bridge to Terabithia*. New York: HarperCollins.

Paul, Miranda. 2019. *Little Libraries, Big Heroes*. Illustrated by Jon Parra. Boston: Clarion Books.

Paulsen, Gary. 2021. *Gone to the Woods: Surviving a Lost Childhood*. New York: Farrar, Straus Giroux.

Pilkey, Dav. 1997. *The Adventures of Captain Underpants*. New York: Scholastic.

———. 2016. *Dog Man*. New York: Graphix.

———. 2019. *Dog Man: Fetch-22*. New York: Graphix.

Pla, Sally J. 2018. *Benji, the Bad Day, and Me*. Illustrated by Ken Min. New York: Lee and Low Books.

Redman, Jess. 2021. *The Adventure Is Now*. New York: Farrar, Straus and Giroux.

Reynolds, Peter H. 2003. *The Dot*. Somerville, MA: Candlewick.

———. 2004. *Ish*. Somerville, MA: Candlewick.

———. 2012. *Sky Color*. Somerville, MA: Candlewick.

———. 2021. *Our Table*. New York: Scholastic.

Rosenberg, Madelyn. 2021. *One Small Hop*. New York: Scholastic.

Roy, Jen Petro. 2019. *Good Enough*. New York: Feiwel and Friends.

Ryan, Pam Muñoz. *Mañanaland*. New York: Scholastic.

Salazar, Aida. 2020. *Land of the Cranes*. New York: Scholastic.

Sendak, Maurice. 1962. *Chicken Soup with Rice: A Book of Months*. New York: HarperCollins.

Sidman, Joyce. 2021. *Hello, Earth! Poems to Our Planet*. Illustrated by Miren Asiain Lora. Grand Rapids, MI: Eerdmans Books for Young Readers.

Silverstein, Shel. 1974. *Where the Sidewalk Ends*. New York: HarperCollins.

Sís, Peter. 2021. *Nicky & Vera: A Quiet Hero of the Holocaust and the Children He Rescued*. New York: Norton Young Readers.

Smith, Sherri L. 2020. *The Blossom and the Firefly*. New York: G.P. Putnam's Sons Books for Young Readers.

Snyder, Laurel. 2010. *Penny Dreadful*. New York: Random House.

Soontornvat, Christina. 2020. *A Wish in the Dark*. Somerville, MA: Candlewick.

Sorrel, Traci. 2021. *We Are Still Here! Native American Truths Everyone Should Know*. Illustrated by Frané Lessac. Watertown, MA: Charlesbridge.

Sriram, Meera. 2020. *A Gift for Amma: Market Day in India*. Cambridge, MA: Barefoot Books.

Stead, Philip C. 2010. *A Sick Day for Amos McGee*. Illustrated by Erin E. Stead. New York: Roaring Brook.

Stevenson, Robin. 2019. *Kid Activists: True Tales of Childhood from Champions of Change*. Illustrated by Allison Steinfeld. Philadelphia: Quirk Books.

Stewart, Melissa. 2019. *Seashells: More Than a Home*. Illustrated by Sarah S. Brannen. Watertown, MA: Charlesbridge.

Strum, James, Andrew Arnold, and Alexis Frederick-Frost. 2009. *Adventures in Cartooning: How to Turn Your Doodles into Comics*. New York: First Second.

Stutzman, Jonathan. 2021. *Bear Is a Bear*. Illustrated by Dan Santat. New York: Balzer + Bray.

Swartz, Elly. 2022. *Dear Student*. New York: Delacorte Books for Young Readers.

Telgemier, Raina. 2019. *Guts*. New York: Graphix.

Thompkins-Bigelow, Jamilah. 2020. *Your Name Is a Song*. Illustrated by Luisa Uribe. Seattle: The Innovation Press.

Tougas, Chris. 2021. *Poem in My Pocket*. Illustrated by Josée Bisaillon. Toronto: Kids Can Press.

Văn, Mượn Thị. 2021. *Wishes*. Illustrated by Victo Ngai. New York: Orchard Books.

Vanderwater, Amy Ludwig. 2022. *If This Bird Had Pockets: A Poem in Your Pocket Day Celebration*. Illustrated by Emma J. Virján. New York: Wordsong.

Venkatraman, Padma. 2019. *The Bridge Home*. New York: Nancy Paulsen Books.

Walt Disney. 1985. *Goofy's Big Race: Walt Disney's Fun-to-Read Library*. New York: Random House.

Warga, Jasmine. 2019. *Other Words for Home*. New York: Balzer + Bray.

———. 2021. *The Shape of Thunder*. New York: Balzer + Bray.

Watson, Renée. 2018. *Piecing Me Together*. New York: Bloomsbury Children's Books.

White, E. B. 1952. *Charlotte's Web*. New York: HarperCollins.

Williams, Alicia D. 2021a. *Jump at the Sun: The True Life Tale of Unstoppable Storycatcher Zora Neale Hurston*. Illustrated by Jacqueline Alcántara. New York: Atheneum Books for Young Readers.

———. 2021b. *Shirley Chisholm Dared: The Story of the First Black Woman in Congress*. Illustrated by April Harrison. New York: Anne Schwartz Books.

Williams, Vanessa. 2020. *Bubble Kisses*. Illustrated by Tara Nicole Whitaker. New York: Sterling Children's Books.

Wiles, Deborah. 2020. *Kent State*. New York: Scholastic.

Winter, Jeanette. 2019. *Our House Is on Fire: Greta Thunberg's Call to Save the Planet*. New York: Beach Lane Books.

Wolkenstein, Evan M. 2020. *Turtle Boy*. New York: Delacorte Books for Young Readers.

Woodson, Jacqueline. 2012. *Each Kindness*. Illustrated by E.B. Lewis. New York: Nancy Paulsen Books.

———. 2018. *The Day You Begin*. Illustrated by Rafael López. New York: Nancy Paulsen Books.

Wang, Andrea. 2021. *Watercress*. Illustrated by Jason Chin. New York: Holiday House.

Yang, Gene Luen. 2020. *Dragon Hoops*. New York: First Second.

Yang, Kao Kalia. 2019. *A Map into the World*. Illustrated by Seo Kim. Minneapolis, MN: Carolrhoda Books.

Yang, Kelly. 2018. *Front Desk*. New York: Scholastic.

———. 2020. *Three Keys*. New York: Scholastic.

———. 2021. *Room to Dream*. New York: Scholastic.

Zhang, Gracey. 2021. *Lala's Words*. New York: Scholastic.

Professional Bibliography

Agency Review. 2014. "An Interview with Lisa Cron." *the-agency-review .com* (blog). May 28. https://the-agency-review.com/cron/.

Allyn, Pam. 2019. "Scholastic Kids & Family Reading Report, 7th ed. The Rise of Read-Aloud." https://www.scholastic.com /content/dam/KFRR/TheRiseOfReadAloud/KFRR_The%20 Rise%20of%20Read%20Aloud.pdf.

Anderson, Laurie Halse. 2019. Keynote Address. Utah Educational Library Media Association's Annual Conference. March. West Valley City, Utah.

Angelou, Maya. 2015. "My mission in life is not merely to survive, but to thrive; and to do so with some passion, some compassion, some humor, and some style." Twitter, August 19, 5:18 p.m. https://twitter.com/DrMayaAngelou /status/634112210143350784.

Arrow, Emily. 2016. "*Poem in Your Pocket*—Emily Arrow." https: //www.youtube.com/watch?v=0xF0nB8ZzXQ&t=11s.

Association for Library Service to Children. 2021. "Randolph Caldecott Medal." https://www.ala.org/alsc/awardsgrants /bookmedia/caldecott. Accessed August 27.

Barnill, Kelly. 2017. "Newbery Medalist Kelly Barnhill." Interview with John Schu. *Watch. Connect. Read.* (blog). February 4. http://mrschureads.blogspot.com/2017/02/newbery-medalist -kelly-barnhill.html.

Barton, Georgina, Margaret Baguley, and Abby McDonald. 2019. "Exploring How Quality Children's Literature Can Enhance Compassion and Empathy in the Classroom Context." In *Compassion and Empathy in Educational Contexts*, ed. Georgina Barton and Susanne Garvis. Cham, Switzerland: Palgrave Macmillan.

Bildner, Phil. 2020. "Guest Post: A High Five for Hope." *100 Scope Notes* (blog). July 25. https://100scopenotes.com/2020/07/25 /guest-post-a-high-five-for-hope-by-phil-bildner/.

Bishop, Rudine Sims. 1990. "Mirrors, Windows, and Sliding Glass Doors." *Perspectives, Choosing and Using Books for the Classroom* 6 (3).

Borovay, Lindsay A., Bruce M. Shore, Christina Caccese, Ethan Yang, and Olivia (Liv) Hua. 2019. "Flow, Achievement Level, and Inquiry-Based Learning." *Journal of Advanced Academics* 30 (1): 74–106.

Braden, Ann. 2018. *Educator's Guide: The Benefits of Being an Octopus.* http://www.curiouscitydpw.com/curiouscitydpw/wp/wp-content /uploads/2018/08/Benefits-Octopus-Ed-Gd-3.pdf.

Candlewick Press. 2012. *A Classroom Guide to Peter H. Reynolds' Creatiology.* https://www.candlewick.com/book_files/0763619612 .btg.1.pdf.

———. 2019. "*A Piglet Named Mercy* by Kate DiCamillo, Author Video." https://www.youtube.com/watch?v=6v6lqxFjSp8.

Castillo, Lauren. 2020. "*Our Friend Hedgehog* Book Trailer." https://www .youtube.com/watch?v=jOL6puSXn9Y&t=4s.

Children's Book Council. 2014. "How Do Stories Connect Us? A Q&A with National Ambassador Kate DiCamillo." January 13. https:// www.cbcbooks.org/2014/01/13/how-do-stories-connect-us/.

Coiro, Julie, Elizabeth Dobler, and Karen Pelekis. 2019. *From Curiosity to Deep Learning: Personal Digital Inquiry in Grades K–5.* Portsmouth, NH: Stenhouse.

Csikszentmihalyi, Mihaly. 1990. *Flow: The Psychology of Optimal Experience.* New York: HarperCollins.

Cunningham, Michael. 1998. *The Hours.* New York: Farrar, Straus and Giroux.

DasGupta, Sayantani. 2014. "Narrative Medicine, Narrative Humility: Bringing Satisfaction and Joy Back to an Ancient Profession." *Creative Nonfiction* 52. https://www.creativenonfiction.org /online-reading/narrative-medicine-narrative-humility.

———. 2018. "Stories Are Good Medicine: Literacy, Health, and Representation." *Reader Leader* (blog). November 5. https://web .archive.org/web/20200606005659/https://bookfairs.scholastic .com/bookfairs/articles/stories-good-medicine.html.

Fagan, Abigail. 2021. "6 Scientific Reasons You Should Be Reading More." *Mental Floss*. April 2. https://www.mentalfloss.com/article/541158/scientific-reasons-you-should-read-more.

Ferguson, Hadley J., and Kristen Swanson. 2014. *Unleashing Student Superpowers: Practice Teaching Strategies for 21st Century Students*. Thousand Oaks, CA: Corwin.

Flasbeck, Vera, Cristina Gonzalez-Liencres, and Martin Brüne. 2018. "The Brain That Makes Us Concerned for Others: Toward a Neuroscience of Empathy." In *The Neuroscience of Empathy*, Compassion, and Self-Compassion, ed. Larry Stevens, and C. Chad Woodruff. Cambridge, MA: Academic Press.

Fox, Killian. 2021. "George Saunders: These Trenches We're in Are So Deep." *Guardian*, January 2.

Green, Andrew, and Simon Bradford. 2011. "Stories of Power and the Power of Stories." *International Journal of Adolescence and Youth* 16 (2): 97–99.

Harvey, Stephanie, and Annie T. Ward. 2017. *From Striving to Thriving: How to Grow Confident, Capable Readers*. New York: Scholastic Professional.

Horn Book Inc., The. 2021. "Calling Caldecott." https://www.hbook.com/?subpage=Blogs,Calling%20Caldecott. Accessed August 2021.

Kaufman, Scott Barry. 2011. "Why Inspiration Matters." *Psychology Today*. https://www.psychologytoday.com/us/blog/beautiful-minds/201110/why-inspiration-matters. Accessed April 2021.

Kim, Aram. 2021. "*Sunday Funday in Koreatown* by Aram Kim." Interview with John Schu. *Watch. Connect. Read.* (blog). February 2. http://mrschureads.blogspot.com/2021/02/sunday-funday-in-koreatown-by-aram-kim.html.

LaRocca, Rajani. 2021. "*Where Three Oceans Meet* by Rajani Larocca and Archana Sreenivasan." Interview with John Schu. *Watch. Connect. Read.* (blog). February 9. http://mrschureads.blogspot.com/2021/02/where-three-oceans-meet-by-rajani.html.

LB School. n.d. "Meet LIFT from Minh Lê & Dan Santat." https://vimeo.com/406975975

Lewis, David, et al. 2009. "Reading Can Help Reduce Stress." *The Telegraph*. March 30. https://www.telegraph.co.uk/news/health/news/5070874/Reading-can-help-reduce-stress.html.

Library of Congress. 2014. "Kate DiCamillo Inaugurated as National Ambassador for Young People's Literature." January 10. https://www.loc.gov/item/webcast-6210/.

———. 2017. "Gene Luen Yang Launches Reading Without Walls Project." April 7. https://loc.gov/item/prn-17-051/.

Lifshitz, Jess. 2019. "Weaving Inquiry into Independent Reading: Using Student-Written Reading Goals to Develop Metacognition AND a Love of Reading." *Crawling Out of the Classroom* (blog). October 9. https://crawlingoutoftheclassroom.wordpress.com/2019/10/09/weaving-inquiry-into-independent-reading-using-student-written-reading-goals-to-develop-metacognition-and-a-love-of-reading/.

Lindstrom, Carole. 2020. "*We Are Water Protectors* by Carole Lindstrom and Michaela Goade." Interview with John Schu. *Watch. Connect. Read.* (blog). April 15. http://mrschureads.blogspot.com/2020/04/we-are-water-protectors-by-carole.html

LitWorld. 2021. "Why World Read Aloud Day?" https://www.litworld.org/learn-more-about-wrad.

Macmillan. n.d. "Reading Without Walls." https://read.macmillan.com/mcpg/reading-without-walls/.

Maillard, Kevin Noble. 2019. "Cover Reveal: *Fry Bread* by Kevin Noble Maillard and Juana Martinez-Neal." Interview with John Schu. *Watch. Connect. Read.* (blog). March 11. http://mrschureads.blogspot.com/2019/03/cover-reveal-fry-bread-by-kevin-noble.html.

Maldonado, Torrey. 2020. "*What Lane?* by Torrey Maldonado." Interview with John Schu. *Watch. Connect. Read.* (blog). May 9. http://mrschureads.blogspot.com/2020/05/what-lane-by-torrey-maldonado.html.

Messner, Kate. 2009. "Authors Who Skype with Classes & Book Clubs." https://katemessner.com/authors-who-skype-with-classes-book-clubs-for-free/.

Miller, Donalyn. 2009. *The Book Whisperer: Awakening the Inner Reader in Every Child*. San Francisco: Jossey-Bass.

———. 2014. "Bless It All." *Book Whisperer* (blog). February 12. https://bookwhisperer.com/2014/02/12/bless-it-all/.

Morales, Yuyi. 2018. "*Dreamers/Soñadores* by Yuyi Morales." Interview with John Schu. *Watch. Connect. Read.* (blog). August 21. http://mrschureads.blogspot.com/2018/08/dreamers-sonadores-by-yuyi-morales.html.

Obama, Michelle. 2020. Watch: Michelle Obama's Full Speech at the Democratic National Convention | 2020 DNC Night 1. PBS News Hour. https://www.youtube.com/watch?v=uKy3iiWjhVI.

Ostroff, Wendy L. 2016. *Cultivating Curiosity in K–12 Classrooms: How to Promote and Sustain Deep Learning.* Alexandria, VA: ASCD.

Penguin Kids. 2020. "*I Am Every Good Thing* by Derrick Barnes & Gordon C. James." https://www.youtube.com/watch?v=CfL2UykcRs4.

Redman, Jess. 2021. "*The Adventure Is Now* Book Trailer." https://www.youtube.com/watch?v=QGiZg3iv8FY.

Reynolds, Peter H. 2020. "*Our Table* by Peter H. Reynolds." Interview with John Schu. *Watch. Connect. Read.* (blog). November 26. http://mrschureads.blogspot.com/2020/11/our-table-by-peter-h-reynolds.html.

Rundell, Katherine. 2019. *Why You Should Read Children's Books, Even Though You Are So Old and Wise.* New York: Bloomsbury.

Rush, Elizabeth Barrera. 2017. *Bringing Genius Hour to Your Library: Implementing a Schoolwide Passion Project Program.* Santa Barbara, CA: Libraries Unlimited.

Ryan, Pam Muñoz. 2019. "Cover Reveal: *Mañanaland* by Pam Muñoz Ryan." Interview with John Schu. *Watch. Connect. Read.* (blog). May 1. http://mrschureads.blogspot.com/2019/05/cover-reveal-mananaland-by-pam-munoz.html.

Salazar, Aida. 2020. "*Land of the Cranes* by Aida Salazar." Interview with John Schu. *Watch. Connect. Read.* (blog). January 7. http://mrschureads.blogspot.com/2020/01/land-of-cranes-by-aida-salazar.html.

Saunders, George. 2021. *A Swim in the Pond in the Rain.* New York: Random House.

Scholastic. 2015. "Booktalk! Top 10 Tips for Coaching the Perfect Booktalk." https://bookfairs.scholastic.com/bookfairs/cptoolkit/assetuploads/161502_bktlk_educator_tips.pdf.pdf.

———. 2021a. "*Allergic* by Megan Wagner Lloyd and Michelle Mee Nutter| Official Book Trailer." https://www.youtube.com/watch?v=Pao6LbVEPyE.

———. 2021b. "*Keep It Together, Keiko Carter* by Debbi Michiko Florence | Book Trailer." https://www.youtube.com/watch?v=LM9GhB7Gt9k.

———. 2021c. "*The Little Butterfly That Could* by Ross Burach | Official Trailer." https://www.youtube.com/watch?v=-Az04fDde8Y.

Sehgal, Parul. 2019. "At 82, Glenda Jackson Commands the Most Powerful Role in Theater." *New York Times*, March 27, 24.

Shelf Stuff. 2020. "*The One and Only Bob* Book Trailer | Katherine Applegate." https://www.youtube.com/watch?v=p8UKRHQ66Mw.

Simon Kids. 2020. "*My Best Friend* by Julie Fogliano, Illustrated by Jillian Tamaki | Book Trailer." https://www.youtube.com/watch?v=3dIB_X7OrIg.

Sterling Publishing. 2020. "Vanessa Williams Presents *Bubble Kisses*." https://vimeo.com/398352521.

Stutzman, Jonathan. 2021. "*Bear Is a Bear* by Jonathan Stutzman and Dan Santat." Interview with John Schu. *Watch. Connect. Read.* (blog). February 12. http://mrschureads.blogspot.com/2021/02/bear-is-bear-by-jonathan-stutzman-and.html.

Svoboda, Elizabeth. 2015. "The Power of Story." *Aeon*. January 12. https://aeon.co/essays/once-upon-a-time-how-stories-change-hearts-and-brains.

Tan, Susan. 2018. "Cover Reveal: *Cilla Lee-Jenkins: The Epic Story* by Susan Tan." Interview with John Schu. *Watch. Connect. Read.* (blog). February 6. http://mrschureads.blogspot.com/2018/09/cover-reveal-cilla-lee-jenkins-epic.html.

Văn, Mượn Thị. 2020. "*Wishes* by Mượn Thị Văn and Victo Ngai." Interview with John Schu. *Watch. Connect. Read.* (blog). August 11. http://mrschureads.blogspot.com/2020/08/wishes-by-muon-thi-van-and-victo-ngai.html.

Vardell, Sylvia M. 2019. *Children's Literature in Action: A Librarian's Guide*. 3rd ed. Santa Barbara, CA: Libraries Unlimited.

Venkatraman, Padma. 2019. "Traveling the World Without a Ticket: Using Global Narrative to Learn About Other Cultures Without Othering Them." *Nerdybookclub.com* (blog). February 1. https://nerdybookclub.wordpress.com/2019/02/01/traveling-the -world-without-a-ticket-using-global-narratives-to-learn-about -other-cultures-without-othering-them-by-padma-venkatraman.

Yang, Gene Luen. 2016a. "5 Questions with Ambassador Gene Luen Yang." Interview with John Schu. *Watch. Connect. Read.* (blog). January 5. http://mrschureads.blogspot.com/2016/01/5-questions -with-ambassador-gene-luen.html.

———. 2016b. "Reading Without Walls Challenge." https://read .macmillan.com/mcpg/reading-without-walls/.

Zak, Paul J. 2015. "Why Inspiring Stories Make Us React: The Neuroscience of Narrative." *Cerebrum* (2). https://www.ncbi.nlm.nih .gov/pmc/articles/PMC4445577/.

#StoryIs

"Story is the gift of a journey into new lands and possibilities."

KARINA YAN GLASER, AUTHOR OF
THE VANDERBEEKERS SERIES

#StoryIs

"Story is the way human beings learn to understand, respect, and love each other."

MEG MEDINA, AUTHOR OF MERCI
SUÁREZ CAN'T DANCE

#StoryIs

"Story is that imagined journey shared between teller and listener."

AIDAN CASSIE, AUTHOR-ILLUSTRATOR
OF THE WORD FOR FRIEND

#StoryIs

"Story is like super glue, like energy, like a LEGO; story connects us."

MADELYN ROSENBERG,
AUTHOR OF ONE SMALL HOP

#StoryIs

"Story is an enchanted mirror that shows us how to live better, more interesting lives."

CHRISTIAN MCKAY HEIDICKER,
AUTHOR OF SCARY STORIES FOR
YOUNG FOXES: THE CITY

#StoryIs

"Story is essential. Story is what makes us human. This remarkable, pulse-raising drive to know the why of things, the who, what, when, where, and how. Story is a compulsion, how we connect to and understand other people."

CAROLINE GERTLER, AUTHOR OF MANY POINTS OF ME

#StoryIs

"Story is change. Every story will change something in us. It could be something as immediate as the mood or an emotion. Or something as long lasting as a mindset or worldview."

MEERA SRIRAM, AUTHOR OF A GIFT FOR AMMA:
MARKET DAY IN INDIA

Be sure and continue the conversation by sharing your own #StoryIs statement on social media.

Credits

Chapter 1

Cover from *The One and Only Ivan* by Katherine Applegate, John Schumacher, and Jodi Carrigan—Illustrated by: Patricia Castelao. Text Copyright © 2012 by Katherine Applegate. Illustrations Copyright © 2012 by Patricia Castelao. Used by permission of HarperCollins Publishers.

From *Good Enough* by Jen Petro-Roy. Copyright © 2019 by Jen Petro-Roy. Reprinted by permission of Feiwel and Friends. All Rights Reserved.

From *The Day You Begin* by Jacqueline Woodson. © 2018 by Jacqueline Woodson. Reprinted by permission of Penguin Random House.

From *Marley Dias Gets It Done: And So Can You!* by Marley Dias. © 2018 by Marley Dias. Reprinted by permission of Scholastic, Inc.

Flora and Ulysses. Text copyright © 2013 by Kate DiCamillo. Illustrations copyright © 2013 by Keith Campbell. Reproduced by permission of the publisher, Candlewick Press, Somerville, MA.

Chapter 2

From *A Single Shard* by Linda Sue Park. © 2011 by Linda Sue Park. Reprinted by permission of Houghton Mifflin Harcourt.

Cover from *The Best at It* by Maulik Pancholy. Copyright © 2019 by Maulik Pancholy. Used by permission of HarperCollins Publishers.

From *Front Desk* by Kelly Yang. © 2018 by Kelly Yang. Reprinted by permission of Scholastic, Inc.

Three Keys by Kelly Yang. © 2020 by Kelly Yang. Reprinted by permission of Scholastic, Inc.

From *Room to Dream* by Kelly Yang. © 2021 by Kelly Yang. Reprinted by permission of Scholastic, Inc.

CHAPTER 3

A Piglet Named Mercy. Text copyright © 2019 by Kate DiCamillo. Illustrations copyright © 2019 by Chris Van Dusen. Reproduced by permission of the publisher, Candlewick Press, Somerville, MA.

Gurple and Preen Illustration copyright © 2020 by Debbie Ridpath Ohi.

Dancing Hands Illustration copyright © 2019 Rafael López.

From *Little Libraries, Big Heroes* by Miranda Paul. © 2019 Miranda Paul. Reprinted by permission of Houghton Mifflin Harcourt.

Our House Is on Fire Illustration copyright © 2019 by Jeanette Winter.

Cover from *Titan and the Wild Boars* by Susan Hood. Illustrated by: Dow Phumiruk. Text copyright © 2019 by Susan Hood. Art Copyright © 2019 by Down Phumiruk. Used by permission of HarperCollins Publishers.

From *Saturday* by Oge Mora. © 2019 by Oge Mora. Reprinted by Permission of Hachette Book Group.

Cover from *The Important Thing About Margaret Wise Brown* by Mac Barnett—Illustrated by: Sarah Jacoby. Text copyright © 2019 by Mac Barnett. Cover copyright © by Sarah Jacoby. Used by permission of HarperCollins Publishers.

From *Carl and the Meaning of Life* by Deborah Freedman. © 2019 by Deborah Freedman. Reprinted by permission of Penguin Random House.

From *Bear Came Along* by Richard T. Morris. © 2018 by Richard T. Morris. Reprinted by permission of Hachette Book Group.

Sam & Eva Illustration copyright © 2017 Debbie Ridpath Ohi.

CHAPTER 4

From *A High Five for Glenn Burke* by Phil Bildner. Copyright © 2020 by Phil Bildner. Reprinted by permission of Farrar Straus Giroux Books for Young Readers. All Rights Reserved.

From *A Place Inside of Me* by Zetta Elliott, illustrated by Noa Denmon. Text copyright © 2020 by Zetta Elliott. Illustrations copyright © 2020

Kent State by Deborah Wiles. © 2020 by Deborah Wiles. Reprinted by permission of Scholastic, Inc.

From *We Are Water Protectors* by Carole Lindstrom; illustrated by Michaela Goade. Text copyright © 2020 by Carole Lindstrom. Illustrations copyright © 2020 by Michaela Goade. Reprinted by permission of Roaring Brook Press, a division of Holtzbrinck Publishing Holdings Limited Partnership All Rights Reserved.

CHAPTER 5

From *El Deafo* by CeCe Bell. © 2014 by CeCe Bell. Reprinted by permission of Amulet Books.

Each Kindness by Jacqueline Woodson. © 2012 by Jacqueline Woodson. Reprinted by permission of Penguin Random House.

From *Fry Bread* by Kevin Noble Maillard; illustrated by Juana Martinez-Neal. Text copyright © 2019 by Kevin Noble Maillard. Illustrations copyright © 2019 by Juana Martinez-Neal. Reprinted by permission of Roaring Brook Press, a division of Holtzbrinck Publishing Holdings Limited Partnership. All Rights Reserved.

From *A Sick Day for Amos McGee* by Philip C. Stead, illustrated by Erin E. Stead. Text copyright © 2010 by Philip C. Stead. Illustrations copyright © 2010 by Erin E. Stead. Reprinted by permission of Roaring Brook Press, a division of Holtzbrinck Publishing Holdings Limited Partnership. All Rights Reserved.

Starfish by Lisa Fipps. © 2021 by Lisa Fipps. Reprinted by permission of Penguin Random House.

Song for a Whale by Lynne Kelly. © 2019 by Lynne Kelly. Reprinted by permission of Penguin Random House.

From *This Way, Charlie* by Caron Levis. © 2020 by Caron Lewis. Reprinted by permission of Abrams Books.

Dreamers. Text and illustrations copyright © 2018 by Yuyi Morales. Reprinted by permission of Holiday House Publishing, Inc. All Rights Reserved.

CHAPTER 6

Is Was Illustration copyright © 2021 by Deborah Freedman.

Cover of *We Are Still Here* by Traci Sorell © 2021 Charlesbridge Publishers. Used by permission of the publisher.

From *Hair Twins* by Raakhee Mirchandani. © 2021 by Raakhee Mirchandani. Reprinted by permission of Hachette Book Group.

Nicky & Vera by Peter Sís. © 2021 by Peter Sís. Reprinted by permission of the publisher.

What Lane? by Torrey Maldonado. © 2021 by Torrey Maldonado. Reprinted by permission of Penguin Random House.

Hello, Earth! (Eerdmans Books for Young Readers) Text © 2021 Joyce Sidman. Illustrations © 2016 Miren Asiain Lora. Reprinted by permission of the publisher.

From *Swashby and the Sea* by Beth Ferry. © 2020 by Beth Ferry. Reprinted by permission of Houghton Mifflin Harcourt.

Sunday Funday in Koreatown. Text and illustrations copyright © 2021 by Aram Kim. Reprinted by permission of Holiday House Publishing, Inc. All Rights Reserved.

Cover from *Bear Is a Bear* by Jonathan Stutzman—Illustrated by: Dan Santat. Text copyright © 2021 by Jonathan Stutzman. Cover art copyright © Dan Santat. Used by permission of HarperCollins Publishers.

From *Where Three Oceans Meet* by Rajani LaRocca. © 2021 by Rajani LaRocca. Reprinted by permission of Abrams Books.

Seven Special Somethings: A Nowruz Story by Adib Khorram. © 2021 by Adib Khorram. Reprinted by permission of Penguin Random House.

Mañanaland by Pam Muñoz Ryan. © 2020 by Pam Muñoz Ryan. Reprinted by permission of Scholastic, Inc.

Our Table by Peter H. Reynolds © 2021 by Peter H. Reynolds. Reprinted by permission of Scholastic, Inc.

Index